Civilization and Enlightenment

Civilization and Enlightenment

THE EARLY THOUGHT OF FUKUZAWA YUKICHI

Albert M. Craig

HARVARD UNIVERSITY PRESS

Cambridge, Massachusetts, and London, England   2009

Frontispiece: Fukuzawa in Paris, 1862. Little more than three years after leaving the Ogata school of Dutch Studies in Osaka, Fukuzawa was appointed an official interpreter of the 1862 bakufu mission to Europe.

Library of Congress Cataloging-in-Publication Data
Craig, Albert M.
  Civilization and enlightenment : the early thought of Fukuzawa Yukichi / Albert M. Craig.

    p.   cm.
  Includes bibliographical references and index.
  ISBN 978-0-674-03108-1 (cloth : alk. paper)
  1. Fukuzawa, Yukichi, 1835–1901.   I. Title.
  LB775.F82C73 2009
  370.92—dc22   2008027462

FOR TERUKO

Contents

Preface

FUKUZAWA YUKICHI was a central figure, and in some respects *the* central figure, in Japanese thought during the second half of the nineteenth century. Accordingly, Japanese scholars have written dozens of theses, articles, and monographs on every aspect of his thought. The challenge to a Western scholar is daunting.

What is new in this book—and "new," to be sure, is a relative term— is a positive assessment of Fukuzawa as a Western as well as a Japanese thinker. This is more than a semantic issue. During an era when contact with the West was new, Fukuzawa dealt with complex Western ideas more extensively and with greater facility than most of his compatriots, and found in them a significance that had escaped their original authors. He used the Western idea of "stages of history" prescriptively to plot Japan's future course, and descriptively to analyze its past and present. In so doing he logically extended Enlightenment thought in a direction unexplored by Western thinkers, and with a greater facility and rigor than any other non-Western thinker. A close comparison of Fukuzawa's writing with his original English text will make this clear.

Most of this book was written at Harvard. I drew on sources at the Harvard-Yenching, Gutman, and Widener libraries, and benefited from conversations with colleagues in the Department of History and the Department of East Asian Languages and Civilizations. I am particularly indebted to the Reischauer Institute of Japanese Studies for its support over the years. This book covers in greater detail one of the three Reischauer Lectures (sponsored by the Fairbank Center for East Asian Research) that I gave in 2004.

My scholarly debts in Japan are many. I studied Fukuzawa while a visiting professor at Keiō University, the school founded by Fukuzawa in 1858, and at the Social Science Research Institute of Tokyo University. Successive directors and the staff at Keiō's Fukuzawa Research Center were unfailingly supportive. I should mention in particular Professor Nishikawa Shunsaku, who generously shared his encyclopedic knowledge of Fukuzawa. I benefited immensely from conversations with Professors Banno Junji, Hirota Masaki, Matsuzawa Hiroaki, and Watanabe Hiroshi. I also fondly remember hours of conversations with the late Professor Maruyama Masao.

Robert Bellah and William Woehrlin read and commented on Chapter 1. I appreciate the support of Kathleen McDermott and Elizabeth Gilbert at Harvard University Press and the help of Julie Carlson, my copyeditor. My sons, John and Paul Craig, read the Introduction and the final chapter and made astute comments. My greatest debt is to my wife, Teruko Craig, who tirelessly read several drafts of the book and made valuable comments.

Civilization and Enlightenment

Introduction

The History of an Idea

This book is about an idea that arose in Scotland during the eighteenth century and then journeyed to Japan, where it became the cornerstone of an ideology for radical change. The idea is that all societies have progressed, or will progress, through stages from "savagery" to "barbarism," and, eventually, to "civilization." During the early nineteenth century, another "enlightened" stage was added to the schema to take into account the progress achieved by Western societies since the time of the original eighteenth-century Scottish thinkers. Nations of the world were ranked according to their position on this ladder of progress, and Europe was at the top. Progress from one stage to the next was not necessarily steady. Some areas of the world were too barren to provide a foothold for development. Even in temperate climes, societies advanced with starts and halts and turns. Yet since progress was grounded in a restless, striving human nature, it could not be denied.

The idea of stages of development arose at about the same time in Scotland and France, but the Scottish stream had the greatest influence on Japan. It is the focus of this study. Because these ideas are so remote from, and in some regards so at odds with, present-day thinking, they are little understood. The first chapter of this book, then, provides a background sketch of their development. It focuses on the transition

1

from John Locke to thinkers such as Adam Smith, Adam Ferguson, William Robertson, and John Millar. Seeing the ideas in the Scottish context will help make clear the very different uses to which they were put in Japan.

The seminal figure in the transmission of these ideas to Japan was Fukuzawa Yukichi (1835–1901). In Japan, he is generally viewed by scholars as the greatest thinker of modern Japan. Fukuzawa was not the only scholar of his era to write of "civilization," but he was the first, the most prolific, and the most widely read.

As a youth, Fukuzawa read Chinese histories. During the 1860s, he read and translated many Western histories and other Western works. From these he took in a Scottish version of the stages of civilization. He used it as a framework within which to organize more detailed patterns of history and as a guide to fundamental historical processes. In his writings, his comparisons of Japan with the West were always buttressed by a rich array of historical examples. When describing an institution or technology, he usually focused on its development.

The second, third, and fourth chapters of the book are about Fukuzawa's introduction of the schema of stages to Japan. Chapter 2 treats his understanding of the concepts of "civilization" and "enlightenment," which he first encountered in American geographies. Chapter 3 presents the interpretation of the stages of history in terms of a "natural philosophy." Fukuzawa came to grips with this philosophy while translating *Political Economy*, a work by the Scottish writer John Hill Burton. Chapter 4 tells how Fukuzawa singled out invention as one of the keys to the attainment of "civilization." Each of the three chapters compares Fukuzawa's translation to the original English sources.

In the course of writing these chapters, I had many questions. Why did Fukuzawa choose to translate one work and not another? What were his criteria? (The issue of choice is clearest when he translated only part of a work.) What did he have in mind in presenting translations to his Japanese countrymen? Was he telling them "This is what Westerners think," or was he saying "This is what is true"? What does it mean when the translation differs from the original English text? Such differences are usually small but significant nonetheless. Had he encountered a cultural problem that language could not bridge? Had he misunderstood the text? Was he trying to present the West in a more favorable light? Apart from a handful of letters, the translations offer the only contemporary evidence of Fukuzawa's thought during the 1860s.[1]

Fukuzawa was a superb translator. He thoroughly understood even the most difficult English texts, excepting a few idioms, and he was a master of Japanese prose. But translation is never a neutral task. The translation of a French novel into English requires slight adjustments for language and cultural differences across the English Channel. In comparison, translating mid-nineteenth-century Western thought into Japanese involved a Pacific Ocean of differences. The East Asian tradition of Japan and the Greco-Christian tradition of the West had had virtually no contact, except for a brief encounter with Iberian Christianity in the sixteenth century and a narrow acquaintance with Dutch medical works in the eighteenth and nineteenth. Translation, consequently, required the creation of an entirely new conceptual vocabulary. Because there are universals in human feelings and institutions, and because these have linguistic equivalents, the task was not impossible. Cultures are usually more miscible than anthropologists like to admit. But at every juncture Fukuzawa had to wrestle with ideas that were foreign to Japan's culture and make difficult decisions about cross-cultural valences. The solutions he arrived at during his translation-writings of the 1860s became the premises of his later original writings. Fukuzawa confessed in his autobiography, "In all of my life the most bone-breaking activity I ever engaged in was translation and writing."[2]

The fifth and final chapter of this book presents Fukuzawa's *Outline of Theories of Civilization (Bunmeiron no gairyaku)*, which was published in 1875. In this book he took ideas from his translations, as well as other Western works, and applied them to Japan. The originality and power of the work lie in Fukuzawa's adaptation of the ideas to fit Japanese circumstances. The adaptation reflects Fukuzawa's genius. The circumstances were also propitious: in an age of change and upheavals, ideas counted and cultural taboos were few. *Outline of Theories of Civilization* may well be the outstanding Japanese intellectual work of the past two centuries.

The Traditional Idea of Civilization

To the Japanese, the Scottish idea of progress was revolutionary because it so totally contravened their conventional wisdom. In Tokugawa Japan (1600–1868), the prevailing worldview was rooted in Confucian natural philosophy. This view had its origins in ancient China, the most isolated high civilization of the ancient world. It held that China was civilized, while those on its borders and beyond were not. The Chinese, for example, called the Japanese the "eastern barbarians," and similarly identified barbarians in the other cardinal directions. China considered itself alone to be civilized because it was the birthplace of the Confucian sages and the center of all learning and culture. It was the self-anointed "middle kingdom," the "central flowery kingdom."

Confucian natural philosophy was concerned with the universe and man's place within it. Especially important was man's ethical nature, which contained moral principles that ultimately inhered in the larger nature or cosmos. By understanding his own nature and by grasping the universal principles that lay within himself, the educated man became capable of moral action; he could act in harmony with society and with the cosmos. As Confucius put it in the *Analects*, "Heaven is the author of the virtue within me." Peoples living beyond the borders of China were considered barbarian because they lacked this deeper understanding of human nature. They might send tribute to China or trade with it, but they were too distant from the wellsprings of culture to master its teachings. Unable to act ethically, they understood only self-interest, profit, and force.

Chinese learning, Buddhism together with Confucianism, entered Japan in the seventh and eighth centuries. The Japanese adapted Chinese ideas to fit their own situation. They ignored the Chinese designation of "eastern barbarians," but kept the concept of "barbarian," using it as they deemed appropriate. The Nara (710–784) and Heian (794–1185) courts, for example, routinely applied the term to the Ezo and other politically unassimilated frontier peoples against whom they launched periodic military campaigns. When the Portuguese arrived in Japan during the sixteenth century, the Japanese called them *nanban* or "southern barbarians," since they had come from the south. During the peaceful Tokugawa era, as schools proliferated and literacy spread, the influence of Confucian teachings deepened, and with it came a keener awareness of the dichotomy between the Confucian and barbarian worlds.

Needless to say, not all barbarians were equally barbarous. Tokugawa rulers recognized that the West had useful practical knowledge when, in 1721, they rescinded the ban on the importation of Western books—except those that dealt with Christianity. In spite of the strict seclusion policy, Dutch merchants were permitted to maintain a trading post at Nagasaki, and in time, schools of Dutch Studies arose, devoted mainly to Western medicine. Since "Dutch" and "Chinese" doctors had different conceptions of disease and competed for patients, each group was highly critical of the other. Fukuzawa's autobiography gives a vivid picture of their mutual animosity. But since medicine had little to do with the central ethical, metaphysical, and historical teachings of Chinese learning, the two rarely collided at a philosophical level. Within Tokugawa education, Dutch Studies was a particular area of what one might call postgraduate study. The small number of students who pursued it had a prior education in the Chinese classics, and they fit their new learning into one corner of its framework. On rare occasions, when a boundary was crossed, retribution was swift. Watanabe Kazan (1793–1841) was a member of a group of Western Studies scholars, who, with conscious irony, privately called themselves the "Barbarian Society." In 1837, when Kazan criticized the Tokugawa government's handling of an incident involving a foreign ship, he was thrown into prison. He eventually committed suicide to shield his daimyo-lord from the taint of his offense.

The arrival of Commodore Matthew Perry's ships in 1853 and 1854 and the treaties that followed posed a conundrum for the Japanese. How could "barbarians" construct steamships and weaponry far superior to theirs? How could Western science grasp principles of nature unknown in China? What kind of barbarians were the Westerners, who had defeated China in the Opium War and had forced the Tokugawa government to abandon its two-hundred-year-old policy of seclusion and sign treaties opening the country? Such questions exercised the Japanese in the years after Perry's arrival and raised grave doubts about the old paradigm. In response, beginning in the 1860s, both the Tokugawa government—the bakufu—and large daimyo domains bought rifles and warships and set about reforming their military according to Western models. At the practical level, they recognized the West's superior technology.

But the intellectual scaffolding for such reforms was rickety. The West, undeniably, had learning of a sort and useful technologies. Sakuma Shōzan, a Confucian scholar with an interest in Western learning, admitted that Westerners were not completely beyond the pale. They had fashioned their science by "investigating things and arriving at their principles," an activity recommended by the great Song Confucian philosopher Zhu Xi. Still and all, they had uncovered only one corner of knowledge. The true test of civilization was in ethics and philosophy, and there, Sakuma avowed, Confucian teachings were superior. In the absence of an alternative conceptual framework, the idea of the West as barbarian, or at least as somewhat less than truly civilized, remained viable.[3]

One Confucian scholar of Edo, the conservative Shionoya Tōin (1809–1867), concluded in an 1846 work that the motivations of barbarous Westerners were akin to those of merchants, who seek only profit. In 1859, he wrote a critique of the Opium War, likening the aggressive British to foxes despoiling the riches of humankind. Tōin's aesthetic perceptions were consonant with his politics.

> [Chinese characters] are evenly balanced and well-proportioned, their shape is luxuriant and graceful, their demeanour is like that of a correct literati, they seem to look backward and aside like beautiful women, they are deftly constructed like golden palaces and jade pagodas, their cast is as faultless as that of precious tripods or sacrificial vessels.

In contrast,

> [Western letters] are confused and irregular, wriggling like snakes or larvae of mosquitos. The straight ones are like dog's teeth, the round ones are like worms. The crooked ones are like the fore legs of a mantis, the stretched ones are like slime lines left by snails. They resemble dried bones or decaying skulls, rotten bellies of dead snakes or parched vipers.[4]

Tōin's rhetoric, of course, was addressing a situation in which the teachings of his lifelong calling were under attack. His livelihood as well as his faith were at stake.

Tōin was not the only one to arrive at such a view. In the society at large, Western letters were viewed with disdain. Verse deriding the al-

phabetic writing of the Dutch aimed at humor, but it also conveyed the
message that the Dutch were at a lower level of culture.

> The cow writes
>   With its slaver
> Dutch letters.
>
> When the samisen string
>   Snaps, it looks like
> A Dutch letter.[5]

Others, too, fell back on Confucian preconceptions. Radical samurai, who sought to drive foreigners from Japan, adopted the slogan "expel the barbarian" *(jōi)*. In their minds, "Westerners" and "barbarians"
were much the same. Nor was the Tokugawa government, despite having been forced to sign treaties and accept an "open the country" policy, immune to such an outlook. The bureau established in 1857 for the
study of Western learning was called the "Office for the Investigation
of Barbarian Books" until 1862.

We might also consider Muragaki Norimasa (1813–1880), one of
three high officials who led a Tokugawa government mission to the
United States in 1860. Muragaki was a man of commendable ability
and sensibility. In his travel diary, he duly recorded his appreciation of
the hospitality of his American hosts. He displayed an interest in technology, and, after visits to hospitals and reform schools, recorded his
shame at the lack of comparable institutions in Japan. In no sense can
he be dismissed out of hand as obtuse or blinkered by tradition. Nonetheless, he reacted instinctively to what he perceived as a lack of re-
straint and propriety in American society. When the leading citizens of
San Francisco gave a banquet in the mission's honor, he compared the
boisterousness of the guests to the drunken behavior of construction
workers at an eatery in Edo. When he attended a session of the U.S.
Congress, he compared the loud speeches and haggling to auctions at
Edo's Nihonbashi fish market. He was appalled when he saw a mummy
in a glass case at the Smithsonian Museum in Washington: "Though
this [exhibit] has come about through their investigation of all things
between Heaven and Earth, it is unspeakable to display the remains of

humans side by side with those of birds, animals, insects and fish . . .
One must call these people barbarians *(iteki)*."[6]

Fukuzawa Yukichi

Fukuzawa Yukichi was born in Osaka in January 1835, the youngest of
five children of a low-ranking Nakatsu domain official. When his father died a year and a half later, his mother took the five children back
to their domain in northeastern Kyushu. Of the 260 semi-autonomous
daimyo domains, Nakatsu was middle-sized, undistinguished, and a
traditional supporter of the Tokugawa shogun. As the son of a samurai,
Fukuzawa belonged to the ruling 5 percent of society, but his family
was at the bottom of what was a steeply hierarchical class. Because of
the father's early death, the family experienced poverty, and Fukuzawa's
schooling began late. When he eventually began his studies, he lagged
behind his classmates but quickly caught up. By his own account, he
was slower than other students in the morning sessions when texts were
read aloud, but quicker than others in the afternoons when the meaning of the texts was discussed. He went on to excel in a curriculum con-
sisting of the Confucian classics and Chinese histories.[7]

   Had Japan's isolation from other nations continued, Fukuzawa
might have ended up as a minor official like his father, or perhaps a
schoolmaster. His low rank, of which he was acutely aware, would have
precluded the attainment of higher office. But the traditional pattern of
his life was broken by events that affected all of Japan: the arrival of
Perry in 1853, the signing of a Treaty of Friendship when Perry returned the following year, and the Treaty of Commerce in 1858. In
1855, a year after Japan's self-imposed isolation had been brought to an
end, Fukuzawa's older brother suggested that he study Western gunnery. Fukuzawa liked the idea; he wanted to make his way in the world
and he was eager to leave the stultifying atmosphere in Nakatsu. At the
age of twenty, he set off for Nagasaki to begin studying the Dutch language. His year there was followed by three years of study at the re-
nowned school of Dutch medicine of Ogata Kōan in Osaka. Here, too,
Fukuzawa excelled, and in his final year he was named the head student
of the school. By his own admission, he was fond of debate and willing
to take on any side of an issue for the sheer joy of argument.

   By 1858, even the backward domain leaders of Nakatsu had become aware of Japan's helplessness in the face of Western naval forces. They ordered Fukuzawa to leave Osaka and open a school at one of the domain's estates in Edo to teach Dutch to its young retainers. His entry into the bustling life at the capital was a critical step in his intellectual development. He tested his knowledge of Dutch against that of famous Edo scholars, and, to his delight, found them wanting. He visited the treaty port of Yokohama, and on discovering that Dutch was of little use, he quickly switched to the study of English. In 1860, he wangled his way into a government mission to the United States as the personal servant of a high official and traveled as far as San Francisco. On his return, thanks to the official and to the abilities he had displayed during the voyage, he was hired by the foreign office of the Tokugawa government as a translator of diplomatic documents. He would keep this position until after the Meiji Restoration in 1868. In recognition of his valuable services, he was made a direct vassal of the shogun in 1864. This was a huge rise in status, one that would have been unthinkable in ordinary times. He again traveled abroad to Europe in 1862, and America in 1867, both times as an interpreter—a lowly but official member of government missions.

During his years at the foreign office, Fukuzawa's life was shaped by changes occurring within Japan. The domains of Chōshū and Satsuma launched a movement to overthrow Tokugawa rule during the mid-1860s. By 1866, domain armies were on the move and pitched battles were being fought. The Tokugawa bakufu found itself caught in a pincers between internal enemies who opposed the treaties and Western powers who insisted that they be upheld. As a translator of diplomatic documents, Fukuzawa had an inside view of the many negotiations with treaty nations. He became a fierce partisan of the Tokugawa cause, at least until shortly before its overthrow in 1868.

While working at the foreign office, Fukuzawa continued to teach Dutch at his little domain-sponsored school. He also began a third career as a translator-author. He added Japanese pronunciations to a Cantonese-English phrasebook he purchased in San Francisco in 1860 and had it published. He translated articles from English-language Yokohama newspapers for private circulation among government officials. Then, in 1864, he began writing *Conditions in the West*, a three-volume work that was published sequentially in 1866, 1868, and 1870. It was the 1868 supplementary volume of this work that first presented an interpretation of the stages of civilization.[8] After the collapse of the bakufu in 1868, he produced a steady stream of translations on a variety of topics and worked at a furious pace to establish himself as an independent writer. Among his translations of 1869 were two additional accounts of the stages of civilization.

After 1870, Fukuzawa entered a new phase of his scholarly life. He continued to read the works of leading Western thinkers, but he abandoned translation in favor of original writing. Broadly speaking, his earlier translations had introduced ideas that he felt were relevant to Japan. His original works applied these ideas to Japan's circumstances. The first works of the new phase were *An Encouragement of Learning*, which was published as a series of essays between 1872 and 1876, and *Outline of Theories of Civilization*, published in 1875. Over the following decades, the evolution of his thought kept pace with his personal circumstances, his wide-ranging reading, and changing conditions in Japan. Even in an era when the number of intellectuals in Japan expanded geometrically, his influence remained large. His little school grew to become the Keiō University of today. He also founded and wrote editorials for *Jiji shinpō*, a major newspaper of the late nineteenth century. His total output was prodigious: his *Collected Works*, in fairly small print, come to twenty-two volumes.

~ 1

The Scottish Enlightenment and the Stages of Civilization

> Man is susceptible of improvement, and has in himself a principle of progression, and a desire of perfection.
>
> —Adam Ferguson, 1767

> Little else is requisite to carry a state to the highest degree of opulence from the lowest barbarism, but peace, easy taxes, and a tolerable administration of justice; all the rest being brought about by the natural course of things.
>
> —Adam Smith, 1776

John Locke and Nature

The European Enlightenment was largely a response to new discoveries in the natural sciences. Galileo and Newton had discovered laws that defined a natural and rational order in the universe. Their theories were central to the scientific revolution of the seventeenth century and convinced European thinkers that they knew more than Aristotle and the "ancients." In the early eighteenth century the "moderns" won the so-called battle of the books. Isaac Newton (1643–1727) was the hero of the day. A huge outpouring of popular works, such as Count Alogrotti's *Le Newtonianisme pour les Dames* (1738), Voltaire's *Elémens de la philosophie de Neuton* (1738), and James Ferguson's *Easy Introduction to Astronomy for Young Gentlemen and Ladies* (1768), acclaimed Newton's discoveries and attempted to explain the new physics in terms that laymen could comprehend.

Inspired by new discoveries about the physical universe, thinkers asked whether a comparable natural order existed in human society, and whether reason could uncover comparable scientific laws in human nature. The writings of Thomas Hobbes (1588–1679), René Descartes (1596–1650), and John Locke (1632–1704), as well as those of Hugo Grotius (1583–1645) and Samuel von Pufendorf (1632–1694), inspired the Enlightenment thinkers of the eighteenth century.

Locke was of particular importance to the Scottish tradition. In 1689, Locke wrote his *Second Treatise of Government*, in which he defined his goal as an understanding of "political power." By this, he meant not actual power, but legitimate power, its character and limits. To define such limits, he needed a ground outside of existing governments on which to stand. Looking to Newton, he found "the state of nature." For Locke, that state became the bedrock condition of man. Before joining together in society, all humans existed in that state and were equal, with rights to life, liberty, and property. He contrasted the natural rights of that original unfettered condition with the actual condition of humans under the existing governments of his age, which usually fell short. To support his conception of man as free and equal in a state of nature, he used both metaphysical and historical arguments.

The metaphysical argument was that God loves humans and must, therefore, have made them free and equal. As Locke expressed it, "the Lord and Master of them all" has not "set one above another," and "all men are naturally . . . in a State of perfect Freedom." The only limit that God has set on their freedom is "the Law of Nature," a law that can be known by reason and "is the *Voice of God*" in man (Locke's italics). It is evident even in these short passages that Locke's argument depends on assumptions about a benevolent deity. Without these assumptions, his assertion that these truths are "self-evident" and beyond question would carry little weight, for, in fact, nothing was less self-evident in the age in which he lived.

Locke's second argument was a conjectural history of early man. Late-seventeenth-century reports from the American continent described peoples more primitive than any previously known to Europeans. Cain had tended his flocks and Abel had tilled the soil, but the American Indian had neither herds nor cultivated lands. Based on these reports, Locke wrote: "In the beginning all the world was America." Since Indians had neither laws nor organization, they lacked the distinctions of rank and property that had arisen in more developed societies. In the absence of such constraints, he reasoned, Indians were individually responsible for their own lives and property. If life or property were injured by another, each individual had the right to punish the transgressor. Locke expressed this by saying that in a state of nature—without laws or police or courts—every man was both judge and executioner. He agreed it was a "strange doctrine."[1]

Living in a state of nature, however, was "inconvenient." The weak could not resist the strong, and life, liberty, and estate were "very insecure." Consequently, in the dim past, men had joined together to form a community or "civil society." Locke admitted that historical documents contained no record of the event, but traces of it, which he referred to as "manifest footprints," were everywhere to be found.

In joining together to form a civil society, men entered a "social compact." They gave up their private right to judge and punish, and in exchange obtained the protection of society. To provide protection, society formed a government, drew up laws, and appointed persons to enforce them. But this did not mean that members of society gave up their natural rights. Quite the contrary, the God-given rights to life, liberty, and property remained more fundamental than manmade civil laws. In fact, the principal function of civil law was to guarantee the protection of these rights. A government was good or bad depending on how well it fulfilled this primary function. A despotic government that oppressed its citizens and offered no protection for their natural rights could properly be overthrown and replaced by one that did. In sum, in Locke's *Second Treatise*, freedom and equality became the touchstones that defined the legitimacy of governments. Most of his great work was written before the Glorious Revolution in which William of Orange overthrew James II, but it was published in 1689, one year after that event.[2]

The Enlightenment was a response to Locke and other political thinkers, as well as to Galileo and Newton. Scotland and France were its principal centers, each influencing the other. French thinkers read Locke, and then Smith, Hume, and Ferguson; Scottish thinkers read Voltaire, Montesquieu, and Turgot. As noted earlier, my study will focus on the Scottish wing of the Enlightenment since it was the formative influence on "civilization and enlightenment" thought in Japan.[3]

Adam Smith

Foremost among the thinkers of the Scottish Enlightenment was Adam Smith (1723–1790). He was born and received his early schooling in

Kirkcaldy, entered Glasgow University in 1737 to study moral philosophy, and then attended Balliol College, Oxford, for a further six years
of study. In 1751 he became a professor of logic at Glasgow University,
and the following year, a professor of moral philosophy. He later traveled in France as tutor to a young duke. He was appointed commissioner of customs for Scotland in 1778 and lived his later years in Edinburgh.

At the University of Glasgow, Adam Smith lectured on four fields:
ethics, political economy, natural theology, and law and society. He revised and published his lectures on ethics as *The Theory of Moral Senti-
ments* in 1759, and his lectures on political economy as *The Wealth of
Nations* in 1776. But he never got around to publishing his lectures on
natural theology or on law and society. It was in his law and society lectures that he expounded his theory of the stages of social development.
Fortunately, several sets of notes by students who took his course on
law and society have been discovered and published.

The earliest stage of human development in Smith's schema was
based on new information about the American Indian. Though Locke
had stated "in the beginning all the world was America," he knew little of it in fact and could only conjecture about man in a "state of nature." Smith, in contrast, could draw on the writings of the Jesuit priest
Joseph-François Lafitau (1685–1740), and extended conversations with
his friend William Robertson (1721–1793), who in 1777 would write
The History of America. Smith concluded that the American Indians represented an earlier stage of development than any previously known in
Europe:

> Among the northern nations which broke into Europe in [the] be-
> ginning of the 5th century, society was a step farther advanced
> than amongst the Americans at this day. They [the American Indi-
> ans] are still in the state of hunters, the most rude and barbarous of
> any, whereas the others were arrived at the state of shepherds, and
> had even some little agriculture. The step betwixt these two is of
> all others the greatest in the progression of society.[4]

Based on the new information, Smith rejected Locke's dichotomous
view of a sudden leap from a state of nature to civil society. Instead, he
wrote that human society had advanced only gradually from the hunting and fishing stage characteristic of earliest man. Others shared this

view. His friend Robertson, in his *History of America*, commented that ancient Greek and Roman writers possessed "only a limited view" of man's "progress through the different stages of society," in that they had never encountered "man in his rudest and most early state."

> In all those regions of the earth with which they were well acquainted, civil society had made considerable advances, and nations had finished a good part of their career before they began to observe them. The Scythians and Germans, the rudest people of whom any ancient author has transmitted to us an authentic account, possessed flocks and herds, had acquired property of various kinds, and, when compared with mankind in their primitive state, may be reckoned to have attained to a great degree of civilization.[5]

What made the difference between the understanding of ancient and modern scholars, Robertson went on to write, was the discovery of America, but even then, "almost two centuries elapsed . . . before the manners of its inhabitants attracted, in any considerable degree, the attention of philosophers."[6]

At the same time that new information about the American Indian was changing his view of early man, Smith also began to perceive that contemporary societies in Europe were achieving economic advances beyond those of any previous age. Smith witnessed the transformation of England and the cities of southern Scotland by commerce and manufacturing, and was concerned to explain how such advances had come about.[7] He then combined descriptions of the primitive, pastoral, agricultural, and the most advanced commercial and industrial societies into a stage theory of history.

In his Glasgow lectures, Smith began with an overview of his four stages:

> The four stages of society are hunting, pasturage, farming, and commerce. If a number of persons were shipwrecked on a desert island their first sustenance would be from the fruits which the soil naturally produced, and the wild beasts which they could kill. As these could not at all times be sufficient, they came at last to tame some of the wild beasts that they might always have them at hand. In process of time even these would not be sufficient; and as they

saw the earth naturally produce considerable quantities of vegetables of its own accord, they would think of cultivating it so that it might produce more of them. Hence agriculture, which requires a good deal of refinement before it could become the prevailing employment of a country.[8]

As society was farther improved, the severall arts, which at first would be exercised by each individual as far as was necessary for his welfare, would be separated; some persons would cultivate one and others, as they severally inclined. They would exchange with one another what they produced more than was necessary for their support, and get in exchange for them the commodities they stood in need of and did not produce themselves. This exchange of commodities extends in time not only betwixt the individualls of the same society but betwixt those of different nations. Thus we send to France our cloths, iron work, and other trinkets and get in exchange their wines . . . Thus at last the age of commerce arises.[9]

He next considered each stage in detail. He emphasized the powerful claims of property and the concern to protect it. It was property, he felt, that determined the nature of law and government. Since in the most primitive hunting and fishing society, beyond personal possessions, there is no property to speak of, that society had no need of regular government. As Smith put it, "Till there be property there can be no government, the very end of which is to secure wealth, and to defend the rich from the poor."[10]

The society consists of a few independent families who live in the same village and speak the same language, and have agreed among themselves to keep together for their mutual safety, but they have no authority over one another. The whole society interests itself in any offence; if possible they make it up between the parties, if not they banish from their society, kill or deliver up to the resentment of the injured him who has committed the crime. But this is no regular government, for though there may be some among them who are much respected, and have great influence in their determinations, yet he never can do anything without the consent of the whole.[11]

The age of shepherds, the age in which "government properly first commences," came next. One of the two versions of Smith's lecture on this subject stresses the role of government as the protector of property:

> The appropriation of herds and flocks which introduced an inequality of fortune, was that which first gave rise to regular government . . . In this age of shepherds, if one man possessed 500 oxen, and another had none at all, unless there were some government to secure them to him, he would not be allowed to possess them.[12]

The other suggests that the severity of law will match the kind of property that is at stake:

> When flocks and herds come to be reared, property then becomes of a very considerable extent; there are many opportunities of injuring one another and such injuries are extremely pernicious to the sufferer. In this state many more laws and regulations must take place; theft and robbery being easily committed, will of consequence be punished with the utmost rigour.[13]

After the pastoral age came the ages of agriculture and commerce. During these ages, laws became more numerous, but the punishments for infractions of laws grew lighter:

> In the age of agriculture, they are not perhaps so much exposed to theft and open robbery, but then there are many ways added in which property may be interrupted as the subjects of it are considerably extended. The laws therefore tho perhaps not so rigorous will be of a far greater number than among a nation of shepherds.[14]

And greater still are the number of laws in the age of commerce:

> In the age of commerce, as the subjects of property are greatly increased the laws must be proportionally multiplied. The more improved any society is and the greater length the severall means

of supporting the inhabitants are carried, the greater will be the number of their laws and regulations necessary to maintain justice and prevent infringements of the right of property.[15]

In these passages, we note Smith's rejection of key components in Locke's thought. He does not speak of metaphysical rights, either God-given or natural. His "age of hunters" resembles Locke's "state of nature" in its lack of formal government, but it differs in that even hunters have dispositions for mutual security. For Smith, the tribal collective was the judge and executioner, not the individual. Furthermore, Smith's model has no dramatic turning point, no social compact, to mark the formation of government and civil society. Instead, he argued that as the "means of subsistence" change, the interests of property owners will lead naturally to the formation of government. Depending on whether the property consists of herds, agricultural land, or commercial goods and manufacturing equipment, different kinds of law will be enacted.

Adam Ferguson

Another Scottish thinker who wrote on the stages of civilization and influenced later nineteenth-century thinkers was Adam Ferguson (1723–1816). Where Smith was economic, Ferguson was social and political. Comparing the two reveals the diversity among Scottish thinkers.

Ferguson was born in a town bordering the Scottish highlands. His father was a Presbyterian clergyman, and, like William Robertson, Ferguson was intended for the ministry. He studied at a parish school, at St. Andrews, and then at the University of Edinburgh, from which he graduated in 1745. He served as deputy chaplain, and then chaplain, to the Gaelic-speaking, pro-British, Black Watch Regiment, where he remained until 1754. In 1757, at the age of thirty-four, he left the ministry to succeed David Hume as keeper of the Advocates Library in Edinburgh. Two years later, he was appointed to the chair of natural philosophy at Edinburgh, and five years after that to the chair of pneumatics and moral philosophy at the same institution. Altogether, he taught at Edinburgh for twenty-six years until he retired in 1785 and was succeeded by Dugold Stewart. He was a member of the Edinburgh circle that included Smith, Hume, and Robertson.

In 1767, Ferguson published *An Essay on the History of Civil Society*.[16] The *Essay* began by describing the general characteristics of human nature—those things that are true of humans in all places and at all times. A few years earlier, Jean-Jacques Rousseau had argued in *Social Contract* (1762) and *Discourse on Human Inequality* (1765) that, potentially, man is most truly human in a "state of nature." Rousseau's *homme sauvage* is self-reliant and lives harmoniously with others, whereas the *homme civilisé* has become dependent on others and alienated from his own higher potentials by the artificialities of "civilization." Ferguson attacked these ideas and, by implication, those of Locke as well, by explicitly denying the conjectural "state of nature." Even early man, he argued, had been a member of a group and was never found alone in nature, and even the most polished civilization was as natural as the rudest savagery.[17]

> Of all the terms we employ in treating of human affairs, those of *natural* and *unnatural* are the least determinate in their meaning.
>
> If we are asked, therefore, Where the state of nature is to be found? we may answer, It is here; and it matters not whether we are understood to speak in the island of Great Britain, at the Cape of Good Hope, or the Straits of Magellan . . . In the condition of the savage, as well as in that of the citizen, are many proofs of human invention; and in either is not any permanent station, but a mere stage through which this travelling being is destined to pass. If the palace be unnatural, the cottage is so no less; and the highest refinements of political and moral apprehension, are not more artificial in their kind, than the first operations of sentiment and reason.[18]

Ferguson argued furthermore that the tendency to improve one's condition is built into human nature.

> We speak of art as distinguished from nature; but art itself is natural to man. He is in some measure the artificer of his own frame, as well as his fortune, and is destined, from the first age of his being, to invent and contrive . . . He would be always improving on his subject, and he carries this intention where-ever he moves, through the streets of the populous city, or the wilds of the forest

. . . If he dwell in a cave, he would improve it into a cottage . . . His emblem is a passing stream, not a stagnating pond.[19]

In this respect, humans differ from animals. In the case of animals, the advancement of the individual from infancy to maturity recapitulates the history of the species. But with man, "not only the individual advances from infancy to manhood, but the species itself from rudeness to civilization."[20]

The middle chapters of the *Essay* deal directly with the stages of society. Ferguson describes these primarily in noneconomic terms, as savage or rude, barbarian or barbarous, and refined, polished, or civilized. These are the terms that were used by most writers on civilization during the nineteenth century. Ferguson understood Smith's economic categories, and by and large accepted them. Savages, humans in their rudest condition, lived by hunting and fishing; barbarians were usually pastoral but might also be agricultural; polished nations were usually advanced in commerce. But Ferguson rejected the economic determinism of Smith, stressing instead the mutual interaction of economic and political factors. Each had its own sphere and a measure of autonomy:

> It has been found, except in a few singular cases, the commercial and political arts have advanced together. These arts have been in modern Europe so interwoven, that we cannot determine which were prior in order of time, or derived most advantage from the mutual influences with which they act and react upon one another.[21]

By "political arts," Ferguson meant the spirit of a people and the level of its civic virtue, as well as the form of government. If a people are vigorous, valorous, and public-spirited, if their sense of community is strong, their nation will be strong. But if a society loses its civic virtues and becomes cowardly and degenerate, or if it pursues wealth for its own sake and determines status by wealth, then it will decline. Such a decline, he insisted, may occur at any stage of development.

The last chapters of the *Essay* focused on the issues of corruption and decline. Not even savage and barbarian societies were completely immune to them. Such a society might be "weak and timorous." Or it might pursue rapine not to enrich the society but as an end in itself. Most savage and barbarian societies, however, were vigorous and bound together by a strong sense of community:

> The bands of society, indeed, in small and infant establishments, are generally strong; and their subjects, either by an ardent devotion to their own tribe, or a vehement animosity against enemies, and by a vigorous courage founded on both, are well qualified to urge, or to sustain, the fortune of a growing community.[22]

Strong states, at a higher stage of development, also might weaken if their civic spirit declined. Many of Ferguson's examples were drawn from his classical education: "The states of Greece, once so warlike, felt a relaxation of their vigour, and yielded the ascendant they had disputed with the monarchs of the east, to the forces of an obscure principality." Rome, too, declined as the internal bonds of citizenship weakened:

> The Roman empire, which stood alone for ages, which had brought every rival under subjection . . . sunk at last before an artless and contemptible enemy. Abandoned to inroad, pillage, and at last to conquest, on her frontier, she decayed in all her extremities, and shrunk on every side. Her territory was dismembered, and whole provinces gave way, like branches fallen down with age, not violently torn by superior force.[23]

The lessons of Roman history carried over to modern times: it is far easier for polished nations to achieve glory than to maintain it.

> The virtues of men have shone most during their struggles, not after the attainment of their ends. These ends themselves, though attained by virtue, are frequently the causes of corruption and vice. Mankind, in aspiring to national felicity, have substituted arts which increase their riches, instead of those which improve their nature. They have entertained admiration of themselves, under the titles of *civilized* and *polished*, where they should have been affected by shame . . . they have fallen prey . . . to the neglects which prosperity itself had encouraged.[24]

Indeed, perfection, even in a free and secure society, may lead to moral decline:

> If national institutions, calculated for the perfection of liberty, instead of calling on the citizen to act for himself, and to maintain his rights, should give a security, requiring on his part, no personal attention or effort; this seeming perfection of government might weaken the bands of society, and, upon the maxims of independence, separate and estrange the different ranks it was meant to reconcile.[25]

In short, Ferguson felt that some measure of danger, hardship, struggle, and risk might be necessary to maintain civic virtues. Duncan Forbes, in his introduction to Ferguson's *History of Civil Society*, notes that Ferguson was the only Gaelic-speaking Highlander among the Scottish philosophers, and suggests that both in childhood and in his regiment Ferguson had personally experienced the internal "bands of society" on which he placed such a high premium.[26] Ferguson was, in any case, far less sanguine about the human condition than Smith, who, despite all of the cautions that he made about wealth, felt that laws, manners, and morality would advance automatically in step with economic development.

David Hume (1711–1776), next to Smith the greatest figure in the Scottish Enlightenment, was halfway between Smith and Ferguson on matters of social causation. Like Smith, he felt that economic development was the foundation of progress and that its consequences were usually good. But like Ferguson, he felt that moral and intellectual factors had an autonomous force. His essay "Of Refinement in the Arts" contains the following:

> [An] advantage of industry and of refinements in the mechanical arts is that they commonly produce some refinements in the liberal; nor can one be carried to perfection, without being accompanied, in some degree, with the other. The same age, which produces great philosophers and politicians, renowned generals and poets, usually abounds with skilful weavers and ship-carpenters. We cannot reasonably expect, that a piece of woolen cloth will be brought to perfection in a nation, which is ignorant of astronomy, or where ethics are neglected.[27]

The ideas of Smith, Ferguson, and Hume were picked up and further developed by a second generation of Scottish thinkers. John Millar (1735–1801), for example, was a student of Smith and Ferguson, and from 1761 became a professor of civil law at the University of Glasgow. In his *Observations Concerning the Distinctions of Ranks in Society* (1771), he described the relationships between parents and children, masters and servants, and husbands and wives at each stage of economic development. Millar was particularly concerned for the condition of women at each stage, a concern that remained important within the Scottish school into the nineteenth century.

Scottish Thought: An Overview

A common feature of all Scottish thinkers was their methodology: they rejected conjecture in favor of facts. Early accounts by travelers to the far reaches of the earth that told of fabulous beasts and strangely configured human beings—one-eyed men and the like—were called into question. John Millar described his method for sifting evidence as "comparative":

> Our information . . . with regard to the state of mankind in the more uncivilized parts of the world, is chiefly derived from the relations of travellers, whose character and situation in life neither set them above the suspicion of being easily deceived, nor of endeavoring to misrepresent the facts which they have related. From the number, however, and the variety of those relations, they acquire, in many cases, a degree of authority, upon which we may depend with security, and to which the narration of any single person, however respectable soever, can have no pretension. When illiterate men, ignorant of the writings of each other, and who, unless upon religious subjects, had no speculative systems to warp their opinions, have, in distant ages and countries, described the manners of peoples in similar circumstances, the reader has an opportunity of comparing their several descriptions, and from their agreement or disagreement is enabled to ascertain the credit that is due them. According to this method of judging, which throws the veracity of the relater very much out of the question, we may be convinced of the truth of extraordinary facts, as well as those that are more agreeable to our own experience. It may even be re-

marked, that in proportion to the singularity of any event, it is the more improbable that different persons, who design to impose upon the world, but who have no concert with each other, should agree in relating it. When to all this, we are able to add the reasons of those particular customs which have been uniformly reported, the evidence becomes as complete as the nature of the thing will admit. We cannot refuse our assent to such evidence, without falling into a degree of skepticism, by which the credibility of all historical testimony would be in a great measure destroyed.[28]

Such methodological considerations led Millar, as it had Smith and Ferguson, to reject the notion of an original presocial "state of nature." Humans, he held, had always been social, for to be so was a part of their nature.

Another assumption of Scottish thinkers was that all peoples, regardless of race and culture, are essentially equal. Robertson, for example, wrote that all humans are born with the capacity to adapt to any level of social advance and are shaped by the society into which they are born:

A human being, as he originally comes from the hand of nature, is everywhere the same. At his first appearance in the state of infancy, whether it be among the rudest savages, or in the most civilized nation, we can discern no quality which marks any distinction or superiority . . . The talents he may afterwards acquire, as well as the virtues he may be rendered capable of exercising, depend . . . upon the state of society in which he is placed. To this state his mind naturally accommodates itself, and from it receives discipline and culture . . . It is only by attending to this great principle, that we can discover what is the character of man in every different period of his progress.[29]

Furthermore, even widely separated societies are likely to be similar at the same stage of development. According to Robertson:

A tribe of savages on the banks of the Danube must nearly resemble one upon the plains washed by the Mississippi. Instead, then, of presuming from this similarity, that there is any affinity between them, we should only conclude, that the disposition and manners of men are formed by their situation, and arise from the state of society in which they live. The moment that begins to vary, the character of a people must change. In proportion as it advances in improvement, their manners refine, their powers and talents are called forth. In every part of the earth, the progress of man hath been nearly the same; and we can trace him in his career from the rude simplicity of savage life, until he attains the industry, the arts, and the elegance of polished society. There is nothing wonderful, then, in the similitude between the Americans and the barbarous nations of our continent.[30]

Still another common assumption was that social development is linear. There may be setbacks; a barbarian people may overrun a more advanced, settled society. But polished societies do not become rude, and commercial societies do not return to the herding of animals. This view was not dogma but a reflection of the information available at the time. In one of his lectures, Smith had asked whether agriculture might not have preceded pasturage among the American Indians. He concluded that, since shepherding was easier, it had not:

> We find . . . that in almost all countries the age of shepherds preceded that of agriculture . . . The whole of the savage nations which subsist by flocks have no notion of cultivating the ground. The only instance that has the appearance of an objection to this rule is the state of the North American Indians. They, tho they have no conception of flocks and herds, have nevertheless some notion of agriculture. Their women plant a few stalks of Indian corn at the back of their huts. But this can hardly be called agriculture. This corn does not make any considerable part of their food; it serves only as a seasoning or something to give a relish to their common food, the flesh of those animals they have caught in the chase. Flocks and herds therefore are the first resource men would take themselves to when they found difficulty in subsisting by the chase.[31]

If history is linear, it follows that even the most advanced present-day civilized societies can see their own past by observing present-day societies at an earlier stage of development. Ferguson wrote:

If, in advanced years, we would form a just notion of our progress from the cradle, we must have recourse to the nursery, and from the example of those who are still in the period of life we mean to describe, take our representation of past manners, that cannot, in any other way, be recalled.[32]

John Millar had a similar view:

When we survey the present state of the globe, we find that, in many parts of it, the inhabitants are so destitute of culture, as to appear little above the condition of brute animals; and even when we peruse the remote history of polished nations, we have seldom any difficulty in tracing them to a state of the same rudeness and barbarism.[33]

Another even more basic assumption concerned progress. Why is it that humans advance and not regress? The Scots agreed that progress could be quickened or held back by social or physical factors. War may deplete a nation's resources. Geography may set limits: great progress is unlikely in arctic or tropical climes. Tartary, Adam Smith suggested, is "unfit by its dryness and coldness" for an advance to agriculture.[34] Within such limits, however, humans possess an inner propensity or restlessness that propels them forward. Smith saw man as an active being with natural and insatiable wants that lead him to improve his material condition: "It is this which first prompted [humans] to cultivate the ground, to build houses, to found cities and commonwealths, and to invent and improve all the sciences and arts which ennoble and embellish human life."[35] Ferguson wrote that even the most refined society is a "mere stage," not a "permanent station," and that man by his nature is a "travelling being." Millar found in man "a disposition and capacity for improving his condition, by the exertion of which, he is carried on from one degree of advancement to another." This disposition leads to "a natural progress from ignorance to knowledge, and from rude to civilized manners."[36] Furthermore, since progress is inbuilt, the succession of historical stages is open-ended; humans will continue to advance in the future as they have in the past. Views not unlike these are still alive in the twenty-first century.

In the context of eighteenth-century thought, was this Scottish view

of history radical or conservative? The best answer is that it was somewhere in between. Anand Chitnis writes:

> [Scottish] thought was highly Whig in tendency. They [the Scots]
> were clearly preoccupied with progress and with the gradual diffu-
> sion through time of political liberty to classes of society hitherto
> considered beyond the political pale. As individuals they were of-
> ten very close to specific reform movements, pressing at the time
> for parliamentary reform or "justice" for the American colonists.[37]

He concludes that the contribution of the Scottish Enlightenment was
to "the evolution of, rather than revolution in, early Victorian industrial society."[38]

Millar exemplified this reformist bent. An ardent Whig, he acclaimed the Glorious Revolution of 1688 and criticized many institutions of his day. Indeed, he was so sympathetic to the early phases of the
French Revolution that some accused him, wrongly, of being a Jacobin
radical. Despite such accusations, Millar's vision of an integrated society actually led him to a cautious approach toward social change. He
warned against a "wanton spirit of innovation":

> The institutions of a country, how imperfect soever and defective
> they may seem, are commonly suited to the state of the people by
> whom they have been embraced; and therefore, in most cases,
> they are only susceptible of those gentle improvements, which
> proceed from a gradual reformation of the manners, and are ac-
> companied with a correspondent change in the condition of soci-
> ety. In every system of law or government, the different parts have
> an intimate connection with each other. As it is dangerous to tam-
> per with the machine, unless we are previously acquainted with
> the several wheels and springs of which it is composed; so there is
> reason to fear, that the violent alteration of any single part may de-
> stroy the regularity of its movements, and produce the utmost dis-
> order and confusion.[39]

Millar's metaphor of a machine was appropriate to the era of invention
in which he lived. He was not, however, implying the existence of master machinists who could, with impunity, bring about sudden changes

in their societies. On the contrary, he was arguing for gradual change through "gentle improvements." Had he written a century later, his metaphor would no doubt have been biological.

To sum up, we might say that prior to the eighteenth century, biblical history and the Crusades apart, most European historians never looked beyond Europe. The rest of the world was viewed as barbarous or dismissed as pagan.[40] Smith, Ferguson, Robertson, and other Scottish thinkers were among the first to look beyond Europe's borders for a comprehensive understanding of the human condition. Their ideas were sophisticated and those who followed in their footsteps extended them further. They began the shift away from kings, queens, battles, and political intrigues, and wrote instead of trade, technology, laws, and institutions; they made history secular and comparative. What Hume wrote about a "piece of woolen cloth" points toward a more modern view of history.

The Scots and Fukuzawa

What were the relationships among Fukuzawa's early works, his English-language sources, and the thinkers of the Scottish tradition? The overview in Figure 1 describes a few of the most important connections in a graphic form. The left-hand column lists Locke, then the leading thinkers of the Scottish school. The arrows leading from one group of thinkers to the next indicate chronology and some intellectual continuity. But just as Ferguson differed from Smith on the dynamics of civilizations, so did thinkers of the Scottish "school" differ among themselves on a variety of issues. Members of the same or overlapping generations usually knew one another. Henry Kames, Hume, Robertson, Smith, and Ferguson were members of the same Edinburgh circle. Millar was a student of Ferguson and Smith. Dugald Stewart was a student of Thomas Reid.

William Hamilton (1788–1856) was a considerable figure in Scottish thought during a slightly later era. He studied at both Glasgow and Oxford, knew Stewart personally, edited the collected works of Reid and Stewart, and succeeded Stewart to a professorship at Edinburgh. Hamilton wrote both on ethics and social philosophy. Despite his prominence, Hamilton is listed here primarily because he was the teacher of

John Hill Burton, whose *Political Economy* so deeply influenced Fukuzawa.[41]

The last category in the left-hand column, "Nineteenth-century ideas of civilization," is intentionally vague. It is included to point out the widespread acceptance of Scottish ideas that led the American geographers Samuel Mitchell and Sarah Cornell to use them in their texts. Mitchell and Cornell may have read the writings of the eighteenth-century Scots, but they are more likely to have picked up the notion of historical stages second- or third-hand from later writings. They clearly read the books of British and earlier American geographers.

The second column lists a few of the specific English-language works that Fukuzawa translated, or in the case of *The Elements of Moral Science*, paraphrased. It focuses on the works that directly shaped Fukuzawa's conception of "civilization and enlightenment" and its philosophical setting. It omits the high-school history texts, gazetteers, and encyclopedias that he used in writing the national histories that are the core of the first and third volumes of *Conditions in the West*. Such works often reflect "Scottish" influences; they took the stages for granted, routinely referring to one society as barbarous and to another as civilized, but since they dealt principally with the particulars of history, they are not included here. The list also omits Buckle and Guizot, who were not Scots and whose influence first appeared in 1875 in *An Outline of Theories of Civilization*.

It was Fukuzawa's intention to translate only contemporary works, for he was keenly aware that knowledge was rapidly advancing. (He translated the Declaration of Independence as a historical document.) Most of the editions he used were from the 1860s, or occasionally, the 1850s. Despite such intentions, some works were older than he thought. Francis Wayland's *Elements of Political Economy* predated Burton's *Political Economy* by more than a decade, and was older still in its ideas. Wayland's *Elements of Moral Science* was first published in 1835; Fukuzawa used the revised 1865 edition for his translation, but it differed little from the original edition, which, in turn, drew heavily on the ethical thought of eighteenth-century Scottish thinkers. Scholars often describe Fukuzawa as an outpost of "Waylandism" in Japan, but one should keep in mind that Wayland was an outpost of Scottish

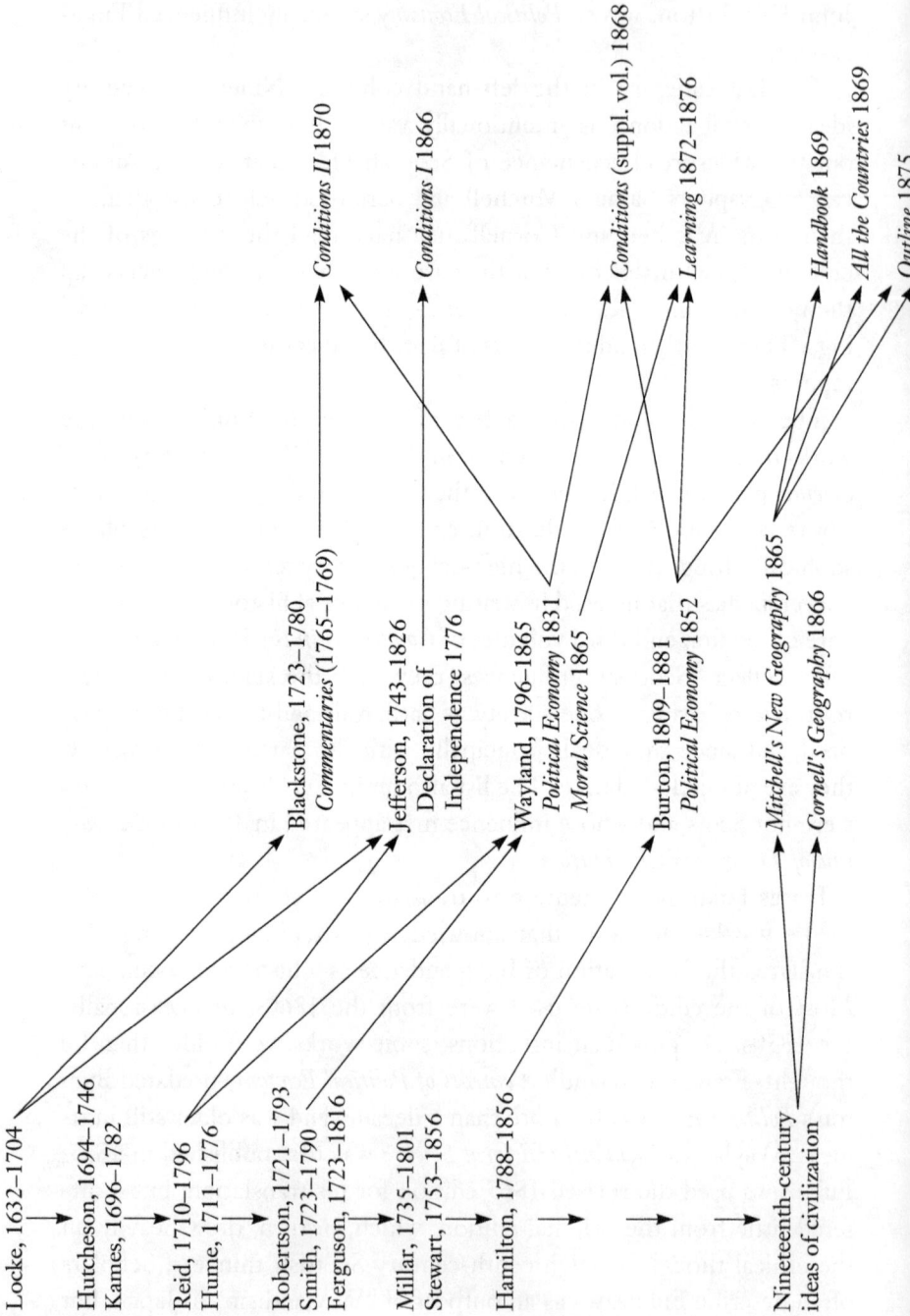

Locke, 1632–1704

Hutcheson, 1694–1746
Kames, 1696–1782

Reid, 1710–1796
Hume, 1711–1776

Robertson, 1721–1793
Smith, 1723–1790
Ferguson, 1723–1816

Millar, 1735–1801
Stewart, 1753–1856

Hamilton, 1788–1856

Nineteenth-century
ideas of civilization

Blackstone, 1723–1780
Commentaries (1765–1769)

Jefferson, 1743–1826
Declaration of
Independence 1776

Wayland, 1796–1865
Political Economy 1831
Moral Science 1865

Burton, 1809–1881
Political Economy 1852

Mitchell's New Geography 1865

Cornell's Geography 1866

Conditions II 1870

Conditions I 1866

Conditions (suppl. vol.) 1868

Learning 1872–1876

Handbook 1869

All the Countries 1869

Outline 1875

thought in America. Wayland's ethics was shaped by the philosophy of Reid and Stewart, as well as by Baptist theology.[42]

Usually, such chronological variation made little intellectual difference. The ideas of the several works cohered sufficiently for Fukuzawa's purposes. The glaring exception was his translation of "Of the Absolute Rights of Individuals," the first chapter in book 1 of William Blackstone's *Commentaries on the Laws of England.* Blackstone wrote his *Commentaries* more than eighty years before the publication of Burton's *Political Economy.* Unlike the Scots, he drew directly from Locke's vision of civil society. Fukuzawa translated the chapter from the *Commentaries* two years after translating Burton, using as his text Robert Malcolm Kerr's one-volume abridgment of the original four-volume work. Published during the 1860s and intended for students, the abridgment eliminated the long passages in Latin and the detailed footnotes of the original. The "Introduction" to the Kerr volume neglected to mention, however, that Blackstone had been born in 1723 and had published his great work between 1765 and 1769. Had Fukuzawa known this, in all likelihood he would never have translated the Blackstone chapter, despite his deep interest in natural rights. Fukuzawa's translation, as always, was exemplary, but the content, reflecting Locke's ideas on early man, was at odds with the ideas in Burton's *Political Economy.* Blackstone, for example, talked of a "social compact," while Burton was quite certain that such an event had never occurred. Fukuzawa translated rapidly and perhaps took only slight notice of these differences.

The middle column ends with the geographies of Mitchell and Cornell. These were critical to the formation of Fukuzawa's conception of the stages. Needless to say, though the authors were well-read and skilled compilers of school textbooks, they were not original thinkers.

The third column lists Fukuzawa's writings in which Scottish ideas appeared. They are placed as near as possible to the corresponding En-

---

(Facing page)   The chart indicates Scottish influences on the early writings of Fukuzawa Yukichi. In this figure, *Conditions* refers to *Conditions in the West (Seiyō jijō),* *Learning* to *An Encouragement of Learning (Gakumon no susume),* *Handbook* to *Handbook of the Myriad Countries (Shōchū bankoku ichiran),* *All the Countries* to *All the Countries of the World (Sekai kunizukushi),* and *Outline* to *An Outline of Theories of Civilization (Bunmeiron no gairyaku).*

glish texts, and, consequently, are not in chronological order. Among the many translations he made during the years between 1866 and 1869, only the three volumes of *Conditions in the West*, the *Handbook*, and *All the Countries of the World* are listed. The two original works cited are *An Encouragement of Learning* and *An Outline of Theories of Civilization*. *Learning* contains paraphrases from Wayland; *Outline* presents a version of the stages that is close to Fukuzawa's earlier translation of Mitchell—along with other new theories.

A final point to bear in mind when thinking of Fukuzawa's early sources is that most of the books in which he discovered Western philosophy during the middle and late 1860s were nineteenth-century restatements of eighteenth-century ideas. He found these books on his own, in bookstores in London and New York, or occasionally in the library of the Gaikokugata (the bakufu's ministry of foreign affairs) or elsewhere in Japan. Only during the early to mid-1870s did he begin to read Buckle, Guizot, Mill, Spencer, Tocqueville, and other first-line thinkers.

~ 2

American Geography
Textbooks

Fortunately for our times, the newest and most assiduous explorers of
human nature have discovered incomparably better means for studying
nations in their various successes according to the circumstances and
conditions through which these peoples, starting from their primor-
dial society . . . rose up to the highest degree of greatness and
enlightenment. Even ancient writers suggested four such conditions of
the human race, of which the most primitive is held to be the condition
of peoples living by hunting animals and feeding on the spontaneous
fruits of the earth; the second is the condition of peoples living as
shepherds, or the pastoral; the third is the agricultural; the fourth and
last is the commercial . . . Such an origin and rising of human society is
common to all primitive peoples, and in accordance with these four
conditions of peoples we must deduce their history, government,
laws, and customs and measure their various successes in sciences
and arts.

—Semyon Desnitsky, 1781

SCOTTISH ENLIGHTENMENT THOUGHT spread from Scotland to
England and the United States, and also to Germany, Italy, and Russia.
During the second half of the eighteenth century, it extended its reach
from universities to a broader swath of educated persons. In the early
nineteenth century, the idea that societies progress through successive
stages of development began to appear in school textbooks and entered
popular thought. By the middle of the nineteenth century, Westerners
universally accepted the schema. In all likelihood, every European and
American whom Fukuzawa met during his travels abroad saw the world
in these terms.

Fukuzawa's first sources for the stages of society and the concepts of
"civilized" and "enlightened" were mid-nineteenth-century American

33

geography texts. Before looking at the specific texts that he used, we might inquire, as a matter of background, when authors of such texts first began to describe societies as "civilized" and "enlightened."

American Geography Texts in the Early Nineteenth Century

Early nineteenth-century American geographies reflect changes occurring within American culture. In 1800, the United States had been in existence only twenty-four years. Half of its population had been born as British colonials. Its high culture was still permeated with elements of biblical fundamentalism that can be traced back to British sources or to colonial times. To the extent that authors of geography texts touched on history at all, they usually attempted to combine the idea of progress with a biblical timeframe. They accepted the biblical account of the Creation and of the events that followed it, such as the Flood. These were facts that they had to address. But they also recognized that the world contained states and societies at different levels of development. They attempted variously to reconcile these two distinctly incongruous sets of ideas.

Jedidiah Morse and Horatio G. Stafford may be taken as representative of the nineteenth-century baseline. In his 1801 *Elements of Geography*, Jedidiah Morse (1761–1826) accepted 4004 BCE as the date of Creation, and speculated that "at the time of the deluge (which happened in the year of the world 1656)," there were 13.7 trillion human beings on earth with a lifespan ten times greater than at present.[1] Most of this population, he wrote, perished in the Flood, and contemporary societies in the world are composed of the descendants of the survivors. Of the several continents, Morse wrote:

> Europe is the smallest, but the most improved and civilized; Africa the most barbarous, and the least known; Asia the wealthiest, the most anciently inhabited, and the theatre of the most interesting events; America the largest, the grandest, as to its mountains and rivers, the least populous and wealthy, the least explored and inhabited.[2]

In Morse's account, America was "peopled early after the flood" but not by "any nation from the ancient continent, which had made any considerable progress in civilization." "Indian tribes" were "but a little advanced from a state of nature."[3]

Horatio G. Stafford, in his *General Geography and Rudiments of Useful Knowledge* (1809), like Morse, tried to fit what he knew of the contemporary world into a biblical timeframe. Of America, he wrote: "It seems probable that the peopling of this continent took place at a very early period, probably soon after the flood; and that man and beasts came hither from Asia." Stafford also accepted the idea of progress and ranked peoples by their level of civilization. He stated, for example, that the early inhabitants of America "consisted of wild and rude tribes, in a savage state of society," and he wrote of "nations advancing toward civilization."[4] But like Morse, Stafford gave no listing of the stages.

The first explicit listing of the stages of society, as far as I could ascertain from the textbook collection at the Gutman Library at Harvard, was in 1819 by Joseph Emerson Worcester (1784–1865). Worcester was born in Bedford, New Hampshire, one of fifteen children in his family, of whom fourteen became schoolteachers. As a youth he worked on the family farm and studied at home. At the age of twenty-one he entered Phillips Academy in Andover, and at age twenty-five entered Yale, graduating two years later in 1911. He had as good an education as could be obtained in the United States in that period. Thereafter, while teaching at various schools, he wrote geographies. In later life he gained fame as a lexicographer, and was the principal competitor to Noah Webster.

Worcester called his text *Elements of Geography, Ancient and Modern.* Under the general heading of "Man," he wrote: "The human species may be considered as existing in the *savage*, the *barbarous*, the *half-civilized*, and the *civilized state.*" Following Adam Smith, Worcester defined each state by its means of subsistence:

In the savage state man subsists almost entirely by hunting, fishing, and the spontaneous productions of the earth. The inhabitants of New Holland and the adjacent islands, a large part of the inhabitants of Africa, and the aborigines of America, are considered as savage.

In the barbarous state subsistence is derived chiefly from pasturage, with some rude agriculture. This state was that of all Europe during the middle ages. It is now the state of that part of Africa which is not savage, of Arabia, and of central and northern Asia.

In the half-civilized state agriculture and manufactures are carried to a high degree of improvement, but foreign commerce exists only in a very limited degree. In this state are Turkey, Persia, Hindoostan, and China.

The civilized state is the most improved form of human society, and exists, though with considerable diversity, throughout most of Europe, the United States, and some other parts of America.[5]

Of the ten American geography textbooks published between 1808 and 1820 that I examined, only Worcester laid out the progression of stages.

Two years later, in 1821, William Channing Woodbridge (1794–1845), in a book titled *Rudiments of Geography*, added an "enlightened" stage to the list.[6] Woodbridge was the son of a teacher and clergyman. He entered Yale at the age of fourteen, the youngest member of his class, and graduated three years later in 1811, the same year as Worcester. He then briefly attended Princeton Theological Seminary, became an instructor at an asylum for the deaf and dumb in Hartford, and, declining an invitation to become a professor of chemistry at William and Mary College, toured Europe for several years. On returning to the United States, Woodbridge published the book.

In a section titled "Civilization," he wrote: "Men are found in five different states of society; the savage, barbarous, half-civilized, civilized, and enlightened." Of the last state, he wrote: "Enlightened nations are those in which knowledge is more general, and the sciences and arts are found in the greatest perfection, as in most of the nations of Europe."[7]

Three years later, in a new book, *Universal Geography, Ancient and Modern*, Woodbridge gave fuller descriptions. Like the Scottish writers, he saw each stage as determined by its characteristic productive forces, and he assumed that literacy, knowledge, and government would advance in tandem with these forces.

The SAVAGE STATE is that in which men gain their support chiefly by hunting, fishing, or robbing . . . They have little knowledge of agriculture, the working of metals, or the mechanic arts . . . A savage claims no private property but his dress, arms, and family . . . They are not accustomed to any fixed residence, and rove, like the beasts of the forest, from place to place, as they are impelled by necessity or inclination.

The BARBAROUS STATE is that in which nations subsist by agriculture, or the pasturage of cattle and sheep, with some knowledge of the use of metals and the mechanic arts. They collect in villages, and have some regular forms of government and religion, but no written language or books.

The HALF-CIVILIZED STATE is like that of the Chinese, who understand agriculture and many of the arts very well, and have some books and learning, with established laws and religion. Still, they treat their women as slaves, usually keeping them in confinement; and have many other customs like those of barbarous nations. They have little foreign commerce, and make few or no improvements in arts and learning. China, Japan, Southern Asia, Persia, Turkey, and Northern Africa, are the principal countries in this state of society.

The CIVILIZED STATE is that in which the sciences and arts are well understood; especially the art of printing; and females are treated as companions. Some nations in this class have advanced no farther, and are considered merely as civilized. They retain many barbarous customs; and the great body of the people remain in gross ignorance; as in Poland, Portugal, and a large part of Russia.

There are others which may be termed enlightened nations, in which knowledge is more general, and the sciences and arts are found in the greatest perfection; as in most of the nations of Europe. All the branches of art and manufacture are carried on in a more skilful, productive, and useful manner, than in Half-Civilized countries, with the aid of machinery, and minute division of labour. Commerce is extended to every quarter of the globe. The political institutions are such as to give greater liberty and more safety than in other countries.[8]

We note that unlike the other four, the "enlightened" category is presented in lower case. Perhaps Woodbridge was unsure of its reception.

In any case, he used these categories throughout his book to explain the behavior of various peoples.

As the schema of stages gained acceptance, the Bible lost ground. A new climate of opinion emerged in which revealed truth was held to be inappropriate to geography texts. This was the beginning of the separation of "scientific truth" from "religious truth," and of the encapsulation of religious belief. Of course, both the authors and readers of geography texts continued to be predominantly Christian, and bits and pieces of the biblical story still found their way into the texts as late as the second half of the century. A discussion of the "family of man," for example, might mention "the first man and first woman." Sketches of the religions of the world, which were also included in the geographies, focused on Christianity, Judaism, and Islam, and tended to bunch together the other, nonbiblical religions as "pagan."

From the 1830s into the 1870s, a listing of stages was a standard feature of high school geography texts. Some texts called the highest stage the "civilized," others called it the "enlightened." The stages of civilization, it should be noted, were presented as an added feature in the geographies, along with short descriptions of the religions, languages, races, and governments of the world. They were usually inserted at the beginning or the end of a textbook that was mostly taken up with a description of the world by continents and countries. Then during the 1880s, texts began to omit the stages. The last geography in which I found the schema was published in 1907. The explicit listing of the stages went out of fashion, but the assumptions on which they rested remained alive. Even during the 1890s and beyond, discussions of the relative achievements of nations and races were couched in terms of their level of civilization. It would not be an exaggeration to claim that the notion of a unilinear progression from savagery to civilization was a standard part of American secondary education for almost a century.[9]

Fukuzawa and the Idea of Civilization

Before turning to Fukuzawa's English-language sources, it will be useful to briefly review the early appearances of "civilized" and "enlightened" in his writings. The first instance was in 1862, when "beschaving," the Dutch word for "civilization," appeared in his *Notebook on My Trip to the West (Seikō techō)*, a small notebook containing the jottings he made while in Europe in 1862. Most of his London notes are in Japanese or English, but right there in the middle of them is "beschaving," followed, also in Dutch, by a list of the five conditions that define civilization. The usual explanation for the Dutch passages is that Fukuzawa jotted down notes at a lecture given by a Dutch doctor in London. I have suggested, to the contrary, that the passage may have come from a Dutch gazetteer. The question remains open.[10] Nor do we know for sure what Japanese term Fukazawa had in mind, if any, when he wrote down *beschaving*. I would conjecture that he had encountered the English word "civilization" earlier, either in diplomatic correspondence, in English-language newspapers published in Yokohama, or during his voyage to San Francisco in 1860.

The second appearance of "civilization" was in 1864, in his early draft of the first chapter of the first volume of *Conditions in the West*. This time he used *bunmei*, which in time became the standard Japanese term for "civilization." The draft began: "In Europe, what is called civilized government *(bunmei no seiji)* combines the following six conditions." His decision to include the list of requisite conditions was no doubt a carryover from his London notes. Whether *bunmei* was his translation of *beschaving*, or whether he had in mind the English term, is not known. Several of the conditions described in the 1864 draft, however, differed from the 1862 list. Where the new elements came from is an open question. Perhaps he based them on his own perceptions of the West. Alternatively, since he had switched to English several years earlier, he may have taken them from some other English work. Also, by this time, he may have read the American geographies.

Another issue is his choice of *bunmei* as the Japanese translation-term. In translating from an English-language work, Fukuzawa's usual practice was to find cultural equivalents in the living language of his day, or, for philosophical terms, in the Sino-Japanese Confucian vocabulary, that would be understood by all educated Japanese. When it came to finding an equivalent for "civilization," however, I would guess that he did not find an appropriate term in the current Japanese vocabulary and that he wanted to avoid the Confucian overtones of terms available in the Sino-Japanese philosophical vocabulary. So he reached back in time and picked a word from the Japanese historical vocabulary that was pleasant sounding and sufficiently appropriate. The *bun* of *bunmei* means letters or pattern and *mei* means light, clean, or bright.

Bunmei had been used as the name of the year-period from 1469 to 1487, "the era in which the Ōnin Wars ended and the shogun Ashikaga Yoshimasa established Higashiyama culture" in Kyoto.[11] The essential point to keep in mind is that Fukuzawa took the Japanese term out of its original historical context and gave it a new meaning in a new intellectual setting.

The publication of *Conditions in the West I* in 1866 furnishes further examples of his handling of terms. By this time, Fukuzawa had read, or had read in, the geography texts by Samuel Mitchell and Sarah Cornell–which I will discuss shortly. Both texts described an "enlightened" stage as well as one that was merely "civilized." To translate "enlightened," Fukuzawa once again reached back into history and chose *kaika*, the name of the Japanese emperor (158–98 BCE) who was ninth in the line that began with the mythical Jinmu. This, too, was not an inappropriate choice. *Kai* means open and *ka* means change; an enlightened age might well be thought of as one that is open and changing. But the selection was arbitrary: the *mei* of *bunmei* means light or bright, so it could just as well have become the word for enlightened, in which case *kaika* might have become the word for civilization.

When he published *Conditions I* in 1866, Fukuzawa himself may have been undecided about how to apply the two terms. The book contained short histories of the United States, the Netherlands, and Great Britain. His source for the history of the Netherlands, *Lippincott's Pronouncing Gazetteer*, used "civilization" twice. The first time, Fukuzawa translated it as *kaika*: "The Batavi . . . probably advanced in civilization *(kaika ni susumi)* by contact with the Romans." The second time, he used *bunmei*: "The Dutch provinces form the most civilized portion *(bunmei no chūshin)* of Europe."[12] Similar examples can be found in his sketch of British history. The English term "enlightened," however, does not appear in any of his English-language histories.

I would further conjecture that by the time Fukuzawa had published *Conditions I*, he already had in mind the composite term "civilization and enlightenment" *(bunmei kaika)* but held back from using it because it was unfamiliar to his readers. Letters he wrote in this period support this contention. In one letter dated 1866/11/07, he wrote to his student Wada Einosuke, who was studying in England, about the political situation in Japan. If an alliance of daimyo is formed, he wrote, "our country's *bunmei kaika* will not advance." In another letter written in the first month of the following year, he expressed optimism about the climate of opinion in Edo, claiming that *"bunmei kaika* is close at hand."[13] Still another piece of evidence may be found in his translation of John Hill Burton's *Political Economy*, which he published in 1868 as the supplementary volume of *Conditions in the West*. In the original English work, the chapter describing man's rise from savagery to better things was titled "Civilization." Fukuzawa translated this with the composite term *bunmei kaika*. In so doing, he followed the American geographies and not Burton, who never employed the composite term.

Fukuzawa's Texts: The Mitchell and Cornell Geographies

Of the American geographies that Fukuzawa read, the most important was *Mitchell's School Geography* by Samuel Augustus Mitchell (1792–1868). Mitchell was the most popular author of school geographies in mid-nineteenth-century America; his texts were used by generations of students. The son of a Scotsman who had come to the United States just three years before the American Revolution, Mitchell began his career as a schoolteacher, but he became dissatisfied with the available geography texts and decided to write his own. For the next forty years he worked with the publishing house of E. H. Butler in Philadelphia, producing geography textbooks, maps, and manuals to accompany them. In peak years, more than 400,000 copies of his primary, intermediate, and high school geographies were sold.[14]

Mitchell's School Geography was first published in 1839 and continued in print through successive editions until 1866. The text is notable for its clarity, and is illustrated throughout with copperplate pictures. Divided into three parts, the first and longest is "descriptive geography," a series of brief sketches, continent by continent, of the important countries of the world. The second part consists of "geographical exercises"—a list of questions about maps in an atlas that accompanied the text. The third is composed of "geographical definitions." The definitions mainly treat topics in physical geography, such as oceans, continents, mountains, deserts, the rotation and revolution of the earth, latitude, longitude, and the points of the compass, but they also include short passages on human geography under the headings "Government," "Religion," "Languages," "Stages of Society," "Political Divisions," and "Races of Men."[15]

A second text Fukuzawa used was *Cornell's High School Geography*.[16] The author, Sarah Sophie Cornell, was born in New London, Connecticut. She began teaching at age fifteen and later served for many years as a public school principal. From the scant biographical information available, it appears that at some point she gave up teaching to become a writer of texts. She joined the American Geographical and Statistical Society and was listed as a "corresponding member" between 1856 and 1860. Had she lived in New York City, she would have been a "resident member." She died in Oswego, New York, in 1875.

The first edition of Cornell's high school text—she also produced primary and middle school texts—appeared in 1856. Most likely it was commissioned by the publisher D. Appleton & Co. to compete with the Mitchell text and others in the lucrative textbook market. Like Mitchell's work, her books became market leaders. The format and content resemble Mitchell's work, but the book is slightly larger, more up-to-date, and even more clearly organized. It has simple, easy-to-read sentences, and, like Mitchell's book, is copiously illustrated with maps, charts, and copperplate pictures of scenes from around the world. In a section titled "The Earth's Inhabitants," the book contains a statement of the stages (Cornell calls them "classes") through which nations pass in their development.

It can be shown that Fukuzawa had both the Mitchell and Cornell texts in his possession in 1866 when he wrote the first volume of *Conditions in the West*. The opening page of *Conditions I* shows several woodblock prints. Two are reproductions of copperplate prints from *Mitchell's School Geography*—a train passing under a stone bridge and a view of Antwerp as seen from across the Scheldt River. The second page has prints of the five races of man from *Cornell's High School Geography*. To these Fukuzawa added the caption: "Within the four seas, one family; the five races are brothers."[17]

In 1868, Fukuzawa drew on *Mitchell's School Geography* a second time while writing the supplementary volume of *Conditions in the West*. In the middle of his translation of John Hill Burton's *Political Economy*, Fukuzawa interpolated his translation of the following passage from Mitchell:

> The inhabitants of the earth amount to about eight hundred and fifty millions, and if they were equally distributed, every square mile of land would contain seventeen human beings.

On an average, a generation of men is supposed to exist about 33 years. Some individuals live more than twice 33 years, and a very few three times that period; but the estimate is, that about 850 millions of human beings are born and die every 33 years; being at the rate of almost 26 millions a year, 70,000 every day, about 3000 every hour, and 50 every minute.[18]

The interpolation helps us date the edition of *Mitchell's School Geography* he used. Printings earlier than 1852 gave lower world population figures, editions from 1866 gave higher figures. Fukuzawa must have used an edition published between 1852 and 1865.

Which of the two geographies had the greater influence on Fukuzawa's conception of the schema? Cornell uses "civilized" and "enlightened" to describe two distinct stages:

What nations are called civilized?
Those that have made considerable progress in the arts and sciences, and manifested some ingenuity and industry in agriculture, commerce, and manufactures; but not equal to the class called enlightened.

What nations are denominated enlightened?
Those nations that have made the greatest attainments in the arts and sciences, and who have displayed most skill and industry in agriculture, commerce, and manufactures.[19]

Mitchell, too, after describing the savage, barbarous, and half-civilized states, does the same. First came the civilized:

How are civilized nations distinguished?
The arts and sciences are well understood, and the people derive their subsistence principally from agriculture, manufactures, and commerce.

What is the condition of the people in some civilized states?
Many of them are very ignorant and superstitious: there is likewise a great difference between the condition of the upper and that of the lower classes of society.

STAGES OF SOCIETY.

Barbarous.   Savage.

Civilized and enlightened. — Half-civilized.

What countries rank among the civilized nations?
Spain, Portugal, Greece, Mexico, &c.

Next the enlightened:

What is the character of enlightened nations?
They are noted for intelligence, enterprise, and industry; among
them also the arts and sciences are carried to a high state of perfection.

How are they otherwise noted?
Females are treated with politeness and respect, the principles of
free government are well understood, and education is more general than among other nations.

What nations belong in this class?
The United States, Great Britain, France, Switzerland, and the
German States.

At the end of his account, however, Mitchell combines the two into a
single stage:

Enlightened and civilized nations are distinguished by the number
and variety of their public buildings and works of national utility;
of these, colleges, hospitals, libraries, bridges, railroads, canals,
&c., are amongst the most prominent.[20]

The frontispiece of Mitchell's work similarly depicted only four
stages: the savage, the barbarous, the half-civilized, and the civilized
and enlightened.
Fukuzawa's composite term *bunmei kaika*, "civilization and enlight-

---

(Facing page) Stages of society. The frontispiece to *Mitchell's New School
Geography* depicts the forces of nature at the center and the four stages of human
society at the top and bottom. Note the American Indian hunting with a bow and
arrow in the sketch at the upper right, the nomad on camelback in the sketch of a
barbarous society, the pagoda and snake charmer at the lower right, and the
Napoleon-like figure to the right of the lady and gentleman at the lower left. In
this picture, the "civilized" and "enlightened" stages are joined.

enment," thus came from Mitchell and not Cornell. There is no hard evidence as to why he made this decision. We may conjecture, however, that Cornell's schema of separate stages would have opened the way for arguments as to which of the two was the proper goal for Japan. Since both stages lay in Japan's future, Fukuzawa probably thought this would lead to confusion. But whatever his reasoning, it is clear beyond any doubt that *Mitchell's School Geography* was the specific source for the term *bunmei kaika*.[21]

HANDBOOK OF THE MYRIAD COUNTRIES

Despite his understanding of *bunmei kaika* as a stage in human development and his use of the term to define the goal for Japan, Fukuzawa did not translate a description of the stages until early in 1869, when he published *Handbook of the Myriad Countries (Shōchū bankoku ichiran)*. The *Handbook* is a short compilation of miscellaneous geographical information such as the size of the five continents, the depths of oceans and heights of mountains, world population, the races of mankind, language families, and the mileage of railroad tracks in each Western nation. Fukuzawa took the data from the geography texts and atlases in his possession.

One entry in the *Handbook* is titled "The Distinction between Barbarism and Civilization" *(Ban'ya bunmei no betsu)*.[22] The entry is based, it turns out, not on the Mitchell work cited earlier, but on a revised and expanded edition, retitled *Mitchell's New School Geography*.[23] Fukuzawa bought the second 1866 printing of this new work at Appleton's bookstore in New York during his trip to the United States in 1867. Like its predecessor, this edition sold hundreds of thousands of copies. Few copies have survived in the United States, and, as far as I have been able to ascertain, no copy is available in Japan. Since the passage in the *New School Geography* dealing with the schema of stages was critical to Fukuzawa's thought and to the formation of civilization and enlightenment thought in Meiji Japan, I quote it in full:

THE STATES OF SOCIETY

Into what two classes may mankind be divided, in respect to their social condition?

Mankind, in respect to their social condition, may be divided into two great classes, viz., Savage and Civilized.

The first named includes all those tribes who have no permanent dwelling, but roam from place to place with their flocks and herds, or in quest of game.

Civilized nations build cities and towns, have durable and comfortable houses, and enjoy the blessings conferred by order, industry, morality, and religion.

How may these two classes be still further divided?

These two classes may be still further divided into five: the Savage, Barbarous, Half-Civilized, Civilized, and Enlightened.

What is meant by Savage life?

Savage life is the lowest stage of existence among wandering tribes. It is but little removed from the life of brutes. Such is the condition of some of the natives of Central Africa, of New Guinea, and Australia.

How do savages live?

Savages roam over a great extent of country, and live by hunting and fishing, and sometimes upon insects, roots, and wild fruits. They make war upon each other, and are very cruel and superstitious. Some savages are cannibals and eat human flesh.

Do savages dwell in houses?

Savages sometimes live in huts of the rudest kind; and a collection of these constitutes a village, where they live for a short time, until their nomadic or wandering instinct prompts them to leave it. They pay little or no attention to agriculture, and are usually naked, or have very scanty clothing.

What is said of their knowledge?

Savages are almost entirely ignorant: they have no knowledge of letters, no system of laws or morals, and no division of land.

How are savages governed?

Savages are governed by chiefs, who are usually absolute and cruel despots.

What is said of the Barbarous state?

The barbarous state is the second stage, not quite so low as the savage. The Tartars, the Arabs, and some North African tribes are in this state.

How do Barbarians live?

Barbarians live in tents or rude houses, which they move about from place to place in search of pasture for their flocks and herds.

What do Barbarians eat?

Barbarians eat the flesh of their flocks and herds and drink their milk. They also pay some attention to agriculture, and raise various kinds of grain for food.

What is said of the knowledge of Barbarians?

Barbarians have written languages, but few among them learn to read and write. Their progress even in the simplest mechanic arts is limited.

How are Barbarians governed?

Barbarians are governed by patriarchal chiefs, called Sheiks, Khans, and other names. These rulers are occasionally very despotic, and their laws are severe and arbitrary. The Tartars, Arabs, and some of the African tribes are of this class.

What is said of the Half-Civilized state?

The Half-Civilized state is a decided improvement, in life and manners, upon the barbarous state.

What are the signs of this improvement?

In the half-civilized state agriculture is conducted with some degree of skill, the useful arts are practised and improved, cities and towns are built and adorned, and a considerable advance is made in learning and literature.

Half-civilized nations, however, are jealous of strangers, and treat their women as slaves. China, Japan, Turkey, and Persia are the principal countries of this class.

What is meant by civilized and enlightened nations?

Civilized and Enlightened nations are those which have made the greatest progress in morals, justice, and refinement, among whom the arts are constantly being improved and the sciences are diligently cultivated.

What great interests are systematically conducted by civilized and enlightened nations?

Civilized and enlightened nations systematically conduct the great interests of agriculture, mechanical industry, and the fine arts.

In this way comforts and luxuries are provided, and the bulk of the people are rendered contented and prosperous. The best examples of enlightened nations are the United States, England, France, and Germany.

Are all such nations equally civilized?

All enlightened nations are not equally civilized. The degrees are various.

In Russia and in some parts of Germany the people are oppressed and ignorant, while the nobles live in luxury. In the United States the people are educated and free, all power is limited by law, and those who live virtuously may live happily.

There are many grades of condition in each of the classes just mentioned. Some nations are more savage than others; some barbarous nations approach the half-civilized state; and among those which are called enlightened, some are much more so than others. The division which has been stated is exact enough for practical purposes.[24]

Fukuzawa's translation of this material for the *Handbook* is lucid and faithful to the original. Several small points may be noted: First, as in the earlier edition, *Mitchell's New School Geography* lists five states of society, although it describes only four. Fukuzawa disposed of the inconsistency by joining the civilized and enlightened into the single stage of *kaika bunmei* and listing only four.[25] Second, Fukuzawa felt the catechism-like format of *Mitchell's New School Geography* was too juvenile for his readers, so he simply presented each stage in one straightforward paragraph. Third, even for so skilled a translator as Fukuzawa, the work had pitfalls. The text states, "Civilized nations . . . enjoy the blessings conferred by order, industry, morality, and religion." In this context, "industry" means "industrious," but Fukuzawa translated it as "industrial" *(kō o susumete)*.[26] Fourth, Fukuzawa removed Japan, but not China, from the list of countries characterized as "half-civilized," a term he translated in this work as *mikai* or "not yet enlightened." Most of his readers probably understood that Japan belonged in the same category. The omission was prudent since the danger of assassination by xenophobes had not disappeared by 1869.

ALL THE COUNTRIES OF THE WORLD

Later in 1869, Fukuzawa prepared a longer geography as a text for Japanese schoolchildren. He titled it *All the Countries of the World (Sekai kunizukushi)*. It was based largely on *Mitchell's New School Geography* and on a new printing of Cornell's work.[27] It is a token of Fukuzawa's

The savage state. *Mitchell's New Geography* depicts the savage state with a battle
scene: five men in loincloths are fighting; three have fallen to the ground.
Fukuzawa added the caption: "A people, ignorant and illiterate, who know only
warfare."

great enthusiasm for the schema of stages that he retranslated the same
Mitchell's New School Geography passage he had translated just months
earlier for *Handbook*. He may have felt a bit sheepish about translating
the same passage twice. In any event, the new and smoother translation
reads like a different text.[28] This time Fukuzawa got "industry" right,
translating it as "industrious" *(kokoro o rō shi)*, and for "half-civilized,"
he used the more literal *hankai* rather than *mikai*. As in the *Handbook*,
he listed China, Turkey, and Persia as examples of half-civilized societies but omitted Japan.

Most of the woodblock prints in *All the Countries* came from *Mitchell's New School Geography;* a few were taken from the new edition of
Cornell's High School Geography and other sources. Mitchell used four
copperplate prints to illustrate the "states of society." Fukuzawa repro-

The barbarous state. Here nomads are shown making temporary camp at an oasis, with their camels hobbled nearby. Fukuzawa removed one camel and several palm trees from the Mitchell print to make room for his caption: "Without permanent dwellings, living in tents, as in Arabia."

duced these prints, affirming their significance as follows: "The pictures shown below, copied from a Western geography, illustrate the development from ignorant savagery to civilization and enlightenment. By looking at these pictures, you will get an approximate idea of the world."[29]

Today these mid-century geographies seem old-fashioned—relics of an age long past. We must remember, however, that they were vastly better than their predecessors. Geographies prior to the 1820s and 1830s were stilted in their writing style, crammed with detail, burdened with speculations based on biblical assumptions, and had few pictures. Those by Mitchell and Cornell were better in every respect.

If we compare these high school texts with the classics of the Scottish Enlightenment, they of course fall far short. They ignore methodology, contain no natural philosophy, and present no analyses of the rela-

The half-civilized state. A Middle Eastern tableau illustrates those who are half-civilized: two men are seated on a divan, one holding the stem of a hubble-bubble tended by a slave boy or servant. Fukuzawa added the caption: "They have permanent dwellings and writing, but their human feelings are unrefined, as in Turkey or in Persia."

tions among law, property, and social class. Nonetheless, they contain echoes of Adam Smith and his successors. While neither Mitchell nor Cornell spoke of "modes of subsistence," both described such modes in terms consistent with Smith. Savages live by hunting and gathering, barbarous peoples are tenders of flocks and have some agriculture, the half-civilized are agriculturalists with some commerce, and civilized peoples possess a more advanced commerce and mechanical industry. As noted earlier, the addition of an enlightened stage to the geographies to take into account new scientific and industrial developments was merely an extension of the original Scottish schema. Furthermore, like the Scottish thinkers, Mitchell and Cornell saw each stage as having a distinct moral and cultural character. It is not just a matter of machine industry; civilized societies are also advanced in their social order, justice, manners, fine arts, and treatment of women.[30]

The enlightened state. Mitchell's copperplate print may be compared with the woodblock print in *All the Countries of the World.*

For Fukuzawa, the chief virtue of the geographies was that they explicitly spelled out the stages of human progress. Most of the English works in Fukuzawa's possession made passing references to "barbarism" or "civilization." But thousands of miles removed from the West, and surrounded by the turmoil of pre-Restoration politics, it is unlikely that Fukuzawa, on his own, would have been able to extract a clear progression of stages from these books. In any case, the geographies were the books he read and they served as his guide. They gave him a skeletal framework for thinking about history in a new way, a framework he used for ordering the detailed historical information he obtained from other histories.

The Four Stages and Japan

Two letters found in Fukuzawa's home after his death in 1901 further illuminate his understanding of the stages. One was an undated letter

文明
開化
の

人ハ書と
して
人情
をととろし
樂とわ
をとあしく

The highest level of civilization is represented by an upper-class Western family, possibly American, which is depicted as happy, harmonious, and engaged in cultural pursuits. The father reads to his sons. The mother plays the piano, the daughter sings, another son dutifully turns the pages of the score. A spaniel sits at the edge of the rug. Fukuzawa removed the pictures and bell-pull from Mitchell's print to make room for his caption: "Civilized and enlightened people read books, are of gentle dispositions, and find many pleasures in life."

addressed to him from Erasmus Peshine Smith. Born in New York City in 1814, Smith graduated from Columbia College in 1832, and from Harvard Law School in 1835. He practiced law in Rochester, New York, for fifteen years, and then taught at the University of Rochester Law School for twenty-one years. In 1853, he wrote a *Manual of Political Economy*. In 1871, at the age of fifty-seven, and on the recommendation of Secretary of War Hamilton Fish, he was hired by the Meiji government as an adviser on international law. He held this position for five years, two years beyond his original appointment. His duties included reading diplomatic correspondence and giving opinions to the foreign minister. He is remembered for the advice he gave in

1872 during the Maria Luz incident, which had international com-
plications. While in Tokyo, he occasionally wore Japanese dress and
strolled about wearing a pair of samurai swords. He returned to Rochester in 1876, and died in 1912.[31] Smith's letter to Fukuzawa was as
follows:

My dear Sir

Every nation whose history we know anything about . . . has
gone through three stages of progress.

1st. That of hunters and fishermen, like your Ainos in Yezzo,
who live on the birds and wild animals, that they shoot or snare in
traps, and on the fish they catch.

2nd. That of Herdsmen and Shepherds, who have tame beasts
. . . They drive these beasts from place to place when the grass of
one pasture has been gnawed away, the beasts are driven to new
pastures.

3rd. The third stage is when men plant grass for their flocks and
herds: dig the ground and cultivate rice and other grains. They
live upon the same piece of land; build houses and fences and have
individual property in land and in beasts etc.

I have not been able to learn that in Japan, you have any history,
or even any tradition, that your people ever passed through the
second stage . . .

It is strange . . . that your ancestors should have jumped from
the first stage . . . to the 3rd . . .

There is another fact. I cannot learn that you have any history
or tradition of Slavery in Japan . . .

I would be glad if you would inform me whether the tradition
. . . in Japan is what I suppose . . .

Yours with great consideration

E. Peshine Smith[32]

A second letter, also undated, appears to be Fukuzawa's response to
Smith's queries. Tomita Masafumi, the editor of Fukuzawa's collected
works, comments that the prose style of the letter was Fukuzawa's but
the handwriting was not. He suggests that it is a copy of Fukuzawa's reply made by a secretary or student. (I have translated relevant por-
tions.)

It appears that the Japanese have not passed through the three stages *(sandan no arisama)* of historical development common to other countries.

From ancient times our people have viewed the eating of animal flesh as unclean. Even today this view persists in the countryside. Horses and oxen were raised, but they were used solely for plowing and cavalry mounts, never for food. And though the word "sheep" is known, from ancient times it appears that they were never raised in any number. Since there was no pasturage, it follows that there was no need to move from place to place in search of new grazing lands.

From ancient times Japan was agricultural. The *Nihon shoki* of 720 CE states: "In the 62nd year of his reign (36 BCE by the Western calendar), the Emperor Sujin proclaimed that agriculture is the base of the country and the livelihood of the people." The chronicle also tells of a pond dug in the land of Kawachi. If a pond was dug, rice was probably cultivated. Sericulture also dates from the ancient past. In the second year of Suinin's reign (28 BCE), it is recorded that 100 rolls of red silk were presented to the king of Mimana.

Thus, though agriculture and sericulture were apparently well established during that era, the pasturage of animals is never mentioned. With agriculture and sericulture, it is also likely that people held private property.

Though we say that the Japanese probably went directly from the first stage to the third without ever going through the second, we find no evidence either in the history following Emperor Jinmu or in tradition that there ever was a first stage on the main islands of Japan. We can only surmise by looking at the present-day Ezo [Ainu] that the main islands of Japan may once have been in a similar state. Be that as it may, since ancient times the Ezo and Japanese have had a different way of life. In 95 CE, in the second year of the reign of Emperor Keikō, Takeuchi no Sukune made a report on his return from eastern Japan: "Among the eastern barbarians is a country called Hitakami where both men and women wear their hair long, tattoo their bodies, and are brave in character. Collectively, these peoples are called Ezo. Since their lands are spacious and fertile, they should be conquered and made our own."

Similarly, when Emperor Keikō ordered his son Yamato Takeru to subjugate the east, he told him of a people called the Ezo among the eastern barbarians: "They cohabit promiscuously and do not distinguish between fathers and sons. In winter they live in pits in the ground; in summer, in caves. They clothe themselves in the skins of animals, drink blood, climb mountains like flying birds and cross fields like the fleetest of beasts . . . They form bands and attack their neighbors, seizing their produce and people. If attacked, they flee into the grasses; if pursued, they disappear into the mountains."

These descriptions of the living conditions of the Ezo people of northernmost Honshu at the extreme boundary of the ancient world were no doubt intended to point out just those aspects of life that differed from the main part of our country. So perhaps the first stage of development of the Japanese people was during the so-called "age of the gods" [the mythical age preceding Emperor Jinmu]. My own opinion on the matter is that by the time Jimmu raised an army in the west to subjugate the east, the Japanese people were no longer at the most primitive stage but had already become settled in their ways.

As for "slavery," from ancient times there is no evidence that it ever existed.[33]

Smith's letter and Fukuzawa's reply shared a common set of ideas. Fukuzawa's response was both reasonable and flexible. He offhandedly consigned the "age of the gods"—an age idealized by traditional thinkers—to the rudeness of savage society. He readily conceded that Japan had never experienced an age of pasturage. (In other writings he spoke of China's influence on the formation of Japan's early civilization, a tacit recognition that outside influences may affect lineal developments.) Smith's queries all dealt with Japan's distant past. Fukuzawa was remarkably knowledgeable about the past; he had read and thought about Japanese classical texts. But his letter strikes us as somewhat detached. Had Smith asked about Japan's future, the response might have been more spirited. What Fukuzawa truly cared about, what he took as his mission, was to persuade the Japanese to move quickly from their "half-civilized" state to one of "civilization and enlightenment."

~ 3

John Hill Burton's
Political Economy

It is shewn by history that nations advance from a barbarous to
a civilized state. The chief peculiarity of the barbarous state is,
that the lower passions of mankind have there greater scope, or
are less under regulation; while the higher moral qualities of our
nature are little developed . . . In that state the woman is the
slave instead of the companion of her husband; the father has
uncontrolled power over his child; and, generally, the strong
tyrannise over and rob the weak . . . In the state of civilization
all is reversed: the evil passions are curbed, and the moral
feelings developed: woman takes her right place; the weak are
protected: institutions for the general benefit flourish.[1]

—John Hill Burton, 1852

Conditions in the West

The supplementary volume *(gaihen)* of *Conditions in the West* was an
anomaly. In 1866, when Fukuzawa published the first volume, which
dealt with the United States, England, and the Netherlands, he planned
to follow it up with a second volume covering Russia, France, Portugal,
and Prussia. He had no intention of veering off on a tangent. But then
he discovered John Hill Burton's *Political Economy for Use in Schools, and
for Private Instruction*, a book published in Edinburgh in 1852.[2] For
Fukuzawa, the book came as a revelation. It seemed to lay bare the assumptions on which Western societies rested; it was as if he had found
a secret manual clarifying everything he had read until then. He broke
with his original plan, put the follow-up volume on hold until 1870,
and instead brought out a translation of a substantial part of Burton's
Political Economy in 1868. He called it *gaihen*, or supplementary volume,
to indicate it was "outside" of his original plan. Along with chapters

from *Political Economy*, the volume included materials from other works to amplify the treatment of points that Fukuzawa wished to emphasize.

In his introduction to the supplementary volume, Fukuzawa explained why he had deviated from his original plan.

> Had I followed the order of the Table of Contents for the entire work given in Volume I of *Conditions*, it would have afforded only a knowledge of the histories, political systems, etc, of each country, and would not have conveyed adequately what Western nations have in common. It would have been like hastily viewing the separate rooms of a house without knowing the structure of its beams, foundation, roof, and walls.[3]

Burton's *Political Economy* added two key dimensions to the description of the stages that Fukuzawa had found in the geographies. First, it added a philosophical dimension: Burton depicted each successive stage of advance as a new unfolding of the potentials in human nature, which, in turn, was a part of the larger natural universe that had been created by God and revealed his intent. Second, where Mitchell and others had merely given thumbnail definitions of the stages, Burton dealt concretely with the transition from savagery to civilization, with examples across a broad range of social institutions and historical contexts. For each setting, moreover, Burton showed how human behavior changed as society progressed from lower to higher stages.

Burton and His Writings

John Hill Burton (1809–1881) was born and educated in Aberdeen, and attended Aberdeen University as a scholarship student. His education there drew heavily on earlier Scottish thought. After graduating, he moved to Edinburgh, where he qualified for the bar. While in Edinburgh, he studied philosophy with Sir William Hamilton (1788–1856), the leading representative of Scottish philosophy during this era. According to Burton's second wife, Burton "attended the course of the late Sir William Hamilton and gained some distinction in the study of moral philosophy and metaphysics, so much that his appointment as assistant and successor to Sir William was seriously considered by himself and others."[4]

Though he had qualified for the bar, Burton's legal practice languished to the point that he was forced to turn to writing for a livelihood. His early output was varied and included anything for which a market could be found—elementary histories, poetry, even "blood and murder" short stories. Over the years, however, his writings became serious: he contributed to the *Westminister Review, Edinburgh, Blackwood's Magazine*, and the *Scotsman*; edited the works of Jeremy Bentham; and wrote a biography of Hume, a *Manual of the Law of Scotland*, and a *History of Scotland*. The last work, published in 1873, established his reputation.

In 1849, while still in mid-career and busily churning out works for income, Burton wrote *Political and Social Economy: Its Practical Applications* at the request of the Edinburgh publishing house of William and Robert Chambers. A comprehensive and densely argued text, it expounded the principles of classical economics. Pleased with the sales of the volume, the same publishing house two years later asked him to write a more elementary text on the same subject for "Chamber's Educational Course." The course included some 150 titles intended for students and persons wishing to improve themselves. Burton contracted to write the text, which he titled *Political Economy for Use in Schools, and for Private Instruction*, and was paid fifty pounds sterling on its completion. It was published in 1852. Burton's name, however, appeared nowhere in the work; the publisher's notice at the beginning of the book merely stated that "the treatise" had been prepared "with the assistance of a writer every way competent for the task." Documents that I discovered in the archives of the Chambers' publishing house, however, leave no doubt as to the author's identity.[5]

Burton's book contains fourteen short chapters that treat what he calls the "social economy" and twenty-two more on the "political economy." The section headings under social economy include such topics as "Family Circle," "Individual Rights and Duties," "Civilization," "Society a Competitive System," "Division of Mankind into Nations," "Origin of Government," and "Education of People." The chapters on political economy treat economics. Burton defined the scope of these two broad divisions as follows:

> Social and political economy are in a great measure blended together; but it may be said generally, that while social economy is

connected with the advance of order, justice, and everything that makes man less an enemy to his neighbor, political economy is connected with the supply of his physical wants, and the enlargement of the material elements of wealth and enjoyment.[6]

In the same notice, the publishers explained why a work titled *Political Economy* contained so many chapters that had nothing to do with the usual subject matter of economics:

Political Economy, as a science reduced to exact principles, is not ordinarily connected with the less authorised definitions of social organisation. But in a school treatise, it is thought proper to depart from this technical distinction. When so much ignorance seems to prevail on the nature of individual duties, and the very foundations of civil society are attempted to be undermined, it cannot but be important to instruct the young in things vital to the wellbeing of states. To present, in simple language, explanations on that hitherto neglected branch of study—Social Economy—is therefore a leading object of the work now submitted to the educator.[7]

Fukuzawa was particularly drawn to the chapters on social economy, a field that he defined at one point as "the study of human relationships" *(ningen kōsai no gaku)*. Of the fourteen chapters on the subject, he translated all but one. Of those on "political economy" *(keizai no gaku)*, he translated only four. In his introduction, he explained that he did not want to duplicate the work of his friend Kanda Kōhei, who had just translated another book on economics.

When Fukuzawa translated *Political Economy* in 1868, he was thirty-three years old. Burton was then fifty-nine. Had Burton known that the work he had written seventeen years earlier was a Japanese best-seller, he would have been astonished, or even bemused. "What will they make of it?" he might have asked.

Two Natural Philosophies

Both Burton and Fukuzawa were primarily concerned with society and politics, not philosophy. Nevertheless, Burton did have a philosophy that accommodated, shaped, and gave coherence to his views. In his translation, Fukuzawa could not separate Burton's views on society from this philosophical setting. He had to come to grips with the philosophy. He had to translate a nineteenth-century statement of eighteenth-century ideas steeped in the Western Greco-Christian tradition into a conceptual vocabulary intelligible to Japanese readers educated in Confucian teachings.

Burton's natural philosophy, like that of earlier Scottish Enlightenment thinkers, excepting Hume and Adam Smith, was influenced by religious belief. He was a theist. After his death, his wife wrote that he had been a member of the Episcopalian "high church." As such, he no doubt accepted biblical revelation as one source of truth. But he was also a natural philosopher. By the conventions of his age, when he wrote about natural philosophy, he could speak of God the Creator and of the nature that God had created, and he could cite the Bible as a historical source, but he could not mention Jesus or appeal to divine revelation. Only deductions from empirical evidence were permitted. These conventions did not hamper Burton since in his natural philosophy the parallelism between God and nature was complete. He could say that nature had wisely implanted a certain tendency in man, or that God had done so, and the difference between the two statements was solely one of nuance. God was the author of nature and his intent could be read in it.

Fukuzawa's natural philosophy is more difficult to pin down. When one views Tokugawa and early Meiji thought in the most sweeping perspective, it is possible to speak of two "secular" enlightenments. The first was the shift from Buddhism to Confucianism during the Tokugawa centuries. This shift was a consequence of the growing number of schools using the Chinese classics and histories as texts, and the consequent rise in the number of literate Japanese. Several types of Confucianism or neo-Confucianism entered Japan: one was Ancient Learning, which argued for the authority of old texts; another was the more metaphysical school of Zhu Xi, which became the Tokugawa orthodoxy.[8]

The second enlightenment was the shift from the nonscientific, Confucian natural philosophy to a science-inspired Western natural philosophy. It began with Dutch Studies in the eighteenth and early nineteenth centuries, and advanced rapidly after the opening of Japan due to the efforts of scholars like Fukuzawa. I would argue that the second enlightenment piggybacked on the first. Had the first "Confucian" enlightenment not occurred, it would have been extremely difficult for Japanese thinkers in the mid-nineteenth century to move directly from Buddhism to nineteenth-century Western thought. It was far easier to go from one kind of natural philosophy to another.

Needless to say, the differences between the Confucian and Western "natural philosophies" are legion. Indeed, in some ways it is misleading to speak of the two philosophies in the same breath. But at a high level of generalization there are a few similarities. Both philosophies (in the form in which Fukuzawa encountered them) appeal to a superordinate authority: God in the West and Heaven in the Confucian worldview. Both address nature—the world, or universe, within which humans make their way. In the Christian-tinged natural philosophy of the Scots, nature is God's creation. In the less dualistic Confucian tradition, nature is in-formed by Heaven. In both, human nature is a part of nature. In both, human nature has higher and lower potentials, with the higher potential being realized through education and moral training or self-cultivation. In both, "civilization" results from the realization of the higher potential by some segment of a population.

Fukuzawa was well equipped to make the transition from the one natural philosophy to the other. His early education in his domain of Nakatsu had centered on the Chinese classics and history. His principal teacher, Shiraishi Tsuneto (1815–1883), was a proponent of the Confucian school of Ancient Learning. Fukuzawa doubtless absorbed some of that school's teachings, though in his 1898–1899 autobiography, our only source for his early life, he speaks less of Shiraishi's thought and more of his criticisms of other scholars. Then, during the second half of the 1850s, Fukuzawa studied Dutch and medicine in Osaka, and in the process he also learned some elements of science. In the early 1860s, he turned to the study of English and to Western works on history, economics, and politics. Because his predecessors in Dutch Studies had first studied the Chinese classics, a fair amount of Confucian terminology, most often that of the Zhu Xi school, had been used in talking about Western science. Science was called *kyūrigaku* (the study of principles, or laws of nature) and the dictum *kakubutsu kyūri* (investigate things and seek their principles) was regularly invoked to sanction Western studies of nature. Fukuzawa picked up these and

In 1860, at age twenty-five, Fukuzawa went abroad for the first time. While in San Francisco he had this picture taken with the daughter of the photographer. In the photo, he wears a simple robe, appropriate to his status as the servant of a high official. He kept the picture hidden until his ship set sail on the return voyage to Japan so that other members of the ship's company would be unable to do the same.

other "Confucian" terms and applied them to human nature as well.[9] He did this not because he was enamored with Confucian teachings—on the contrary, he felt they were old-fashioned and ridiculed them at every turn—but because they were the terms he knew and because they were the only terms available to him that sufficed for the translation of the concepts in his English sources. He used this Confucian vocabulary in new contexts and with new meanings, but the original associations of the terms, in small ways, nonetheless influenced his understanding of the Western concepts. How this happened will be clear in the selections that follow.

The Basics: Human Nature, God, and the Family

Burton began *Political Economy* by laying out the ABC's of his worldview. Simply put, human beings were fashioned so that they might get along in the world.

> Man, in being placed upon the earth by his Divine Creator, has been invested with certain powers and dispositions which bear a relation to the qualities of the external world, and appear as designed to enable him to live and thrive in this transient scene of being.[10]

But the earth is no Garden of Eden. It challenges man.

> His happiness, as far as that scene of existence is concerned, depends on the success with which he can adapt himself to each accidental circumstance as it arises, and the skill with which he applies himself to the improvement of those circumstances. He is not offered ready means of indulgence, but called on to observe that, by a due degree of mental and bodily exertion, he may supply himself with what will satisfy his wants and gratify his tastes. This is simply equivalent to an intimation from above, that he is designed to be AN ACTIVE BEING. He must *work* that he may *enjoy*. Even the physical evils with which he is surrounded appear as part of the appointed means for sustaining the activity of the wonderful machine forming the human constitution. We struggle with difficulties and good results from the struggle.[11]

These passages confronted Fukuzawa with the problem of translating the Western concept of deity into Japanese. One solution was to use *ten* or "heaven." In the passage above, he rendered "Divine Creator" as *ten*. (Elsewhere he also used a variety of Confucian terms containing the *ten* ideograph—such as *tendō* or the "Way of Heaven," *tennen,* "natural," and *tenpu,* "a gift from heaven.") Another solution was to translate "Divine Creator" literally as "the master of creation" *(zōbutsushu).*[12] Neither translation was wholly satisfactory, however. The Confucian heaven or *ten* was not transcendental enough to convey the Western sense of deity, and *zōbutsushu* was too foreign-sounding a word.[13] Fukuzawa alternated between the two solutions to give his readers a sense of the original English.

The same problem arose in Burton's treatment of marriage and the family.

> The married life is evidently productive of happiness, and tends to the good of society. Among the lower animals, wherever the young are at once independent of the parent, there is no pairing; wherever the progeny are brought into the world in a tender state, requiring the care of both parents, there the pairing arrangement exists, however temporary. It is therefore much more likely to be the dictate of nature or appointment of God, than any opposite arrangement. The young of the human race are delicate in infancy, and remain long in that state; there, accordingly, the marriage state is peculiarly called for, and there, we may be assured, the tendency to it has been planted by nature with peculiar care.[14]

Thus, in the family altruism is the rule:

> As a direct consequence of the natural affections, human beings are deeply interested in the nurture, protection, and general well-being of their offspring. The rule of nature is, that the parent has no selfishness towards a child . . . As against all the rest of the world, he is a rival and to some extent a self-seeker; but within the home circle no such feelings enter. A divine benevolence and kindliness shine there, as if foreshadowing some better condition of humanity yet to come.[15]

In rendering these passages, one can only imagine the difficulties posed for even so adept a translator as Fukuzawa. When Burton wrote "dictate of nature or appointment of God," he did not mean one or the other. He meant both. By putting the two side by side, he strength-ened his approval of married life. The Declaration of Independence ex-pressed the same dualism in the words "the equal station to which the laws of nature and nature's God entitled them." In his 1866 translation of the Declaration, Fukuzawa tried to convey the dualism with *butsuri tendō* (the principles of things and the way of heaven). But in translat-ing Burton, Fukuzawa threw up his hands, abandoned the dualism, and wrote simply, "this was brought about by heaven *(ten)*." He under-stood perfectly what Burton meant by "any opposite arrangement," and wrote "not by human efforts *(jinryoku ni arazu)*."

Once he understood that Burton used God and nature almost inter-changeably, Fukuzawa allowed himself the same leeway. For the sen-tence describing the marriage state as having been "planted by nature with peculiar care," he translated "nature" as "the Creator" *(zōbutsu-shu)*. And when Burton wrote that it is a "rule of nature" for men and women to marry, Fukuzawa rendered "rule of nature" as "the great way of heaven *(ten no daidō)*." For "divine benevolence," he wrote "the deep intent of the Creator" *(zōbutsushu no shin'i)*. Though different in nu-ance, none of these translations miss the mark.[16]

There still remains an epistemological issue. However much Burton smuggled Christian morality into his natural philosophy, he felt con-strained to present his findings as empirical data and not as axiomatic moral principles. So when he spoke of married life as "productive of happiness," he inserted qualifiers that pointed up the tentativeness of empirical knowledge: "evidently," "tends to," "is more likely." Fuku-zawa was uncomfortable with the tentativeness of these terms. Was it that his earlier Confucian education led him to think in terms of fixed moral principles? Whatever the reason, he dropped all the qualifiers and wrote of married life as "the great moral principle *(dairin)*."

Society

With the basics taken care of, Burton turned to society, and presented arguments that would further shape Fukuzawa's interpretation of civili-zation. In Burton's analysis, societies had three salient features: they were natural, competitive, and exhibited different patterns of behavior according to the stage of their civilization. On the first point, he wrote:

It is not more of a dictate of nature *(ten no michi)* that the man and
the woman should form the little community called the family,
than that numbers of men and women should associate for the
forming of more extensive societies, under the names of nations or
states. Some animals are solitary in their habits . . . others are gre-
garious . . . By a like impulse, man is social *(sono tenpin gunkyo o
konomi)*; he both has an enjoyment in the society of his fellow-
creatures, and, by association, can effect many good ends for his
own advantage, which could not be attained otherwise.[17]

In this passage, Burton aligns himself with his Scottish predecessors
and against Locke and Blackstone. He argues, implicitly at least, that
since humans are social by nature, there never existed a presocial "state
of nature" and that, consequently, there was never a need for humans
to join in a "social compact."[18]

Burton treated competition, a second feature of society, in a chapter
titled "Society a Competitive System." It began:

The disinterested affection and the willingness to make sacrifices
for each other, which are characteristic of the family circle, do not
follow men beyond it into the ordinary intercourse of the world:
there each pursues his own course, relies on his own efforts, and
endeavors to accomplish his own objects. In doing so, all compete
less or more with each other. Hence society at large is said to be
formed on the competitive principle. It is much to the advantage
of human nature that it should be so, since, were there not emulation among mankind, and motives for individual exertion, many
valuable services would fail to be performed.[19]

Thus, competition is not only natural but good. Lest there be any
doubt about this—some nineteenth-century Western thinkers thought
otherwise—Burton suggested that the innate competitiveness of humans was a part of God's plan: "Emulation and a well-directed ambi-
tion seem wisely implanted in man for the welfare of society." Fukuzawa dropped the "seem" and translated "wisely implanted" as: "All of
this is brought about by the Creator and informs us of the fineness of
his intent." *(Minna kore zōbutsushu no shikarashimuru tokoro ni te, sono
shinshō no takumi naru koto shirubeshi.)*[20]

Competition took different forms, depending on the society's level of civilization.

> In rude and imperfect states of society *(fubun fumei no yo)* . . . man . . . aggrandizes himself at the expense of others; sometimes by conquest and rapine, the conquerors being robbers on a grand scale; sometimes it is by forcing men to be slaves, or, in other words, compelling them by force to give up the fruit of their labour.
>
> But it is quite otherwise when men's natures are purified, and their faculties developed by cultivation *(hitobito tokkō o osame chishiki o migaku ni itarite)*. In a state of civilization, a man in advancing himself, benefits his species . . . He does not become affluent by seizing on what other people have produced, but by himself producing.[21]

In the autobiography he wrote shortly before his death, Fukuzawa tells of an incident in the 1860s when he translated the table of contents of *Political Economy* for a high official of the Tokugawa treasury. The official objected to Fukuzawa's use of *kyōsō* (literally, compete and struggle) in his translation of the chapter title "Society a Competitive System." The official conceded that merchants did in fact struggle in a race for profits, but objected to the translation on the grounds that the ideograph "struggle" *(sō* or *arasou)* was not "peaceful sounding" *(odayaka de nai)*. Fukuzawa replied to the official that he would ink out the offending term since there was no other way to translate it. He further commented in the autobiography that this one incident revealed the despicable spirit of the Tokugawa government as a whole. In 1868, however, Fukuzawa found a less provocative way of translating the term.[22]

Civilization

Although Burton contrasted rude and refined societies throughout *Political Economy*, he dealt with the issue more systematically in a chapter titled "Civilization," which, as we have noted, Fukuzawa translated as "Civilization and Enlightenment." Burton's interpretation used much the same vocabulary as the American geographies, but unlike the geographies' modal characterizations of discrete stages, he portrayed a spectrum that stretched from the savage or barbarous to the civilized.

One rule of thumb Burton used in writing about societies and civilizations is that the natural is good and the artificial bad. By artificial, he meant behavior or institutions that go against nature. But how did he apply this rule to savage and civilized societies? Were not savages and barbarians more "natural" than their civilized descendants?

> It has also been asserted by some that the barbarous state is natural *(tennen)* while that of civilization is artificial *(jin'i):* but the word artificial is here misused. The qualities which men shew in civilization are as natural as those shewn in barbarism. Their going on to the forms of civilization, to its institutions, and to a submission to its mild restraints, is purely a result of their inherent dispositions; and it might perhaps be shewn, that though a primitive barbarism is natural, to remain in it is not so, but can only be the result of some external interference.[23]

For Burton, then, civilization is "as natural" as primitive barbarism. So far, so good. But that was not enough. He wanted civilization, somehow, to be better than the primitive state. To make this point, he began by discerning higher and lower faculties within human nature. The "lower passions" hold sway in savage or barbarous societies, where "the woman is the slave instead of the companion of her husband" and where "the strong tyrannise . . . the weak." But "in the state of civilization all is reversed: the evil passions are curbed and the moral feelings developed: woman takes her right place; the weak are protected."[24] Thus civilization is indisputably better, even if only "as natural."

Because Rousseau and others had answered the question differently, Burton felt obliged to provide further arguments in support of his position. Savages may wander their deserts with "unbounded freedom," but in fact they possessed solely "a freedom to starve." Only after civilization has imposed equal laws does "true freedom" appear. Savages are filthy, and cleanliness, which "no one would say . . . is not a natural feeling," comes with civilization. In the savage state "the natural inclination to cleanliness" lies, "like an intellectual faculty in an infant, undeveloped." Nor are savages entirely free from the artificial. Some tribes bind boards to the heads of infants to make them flat. Or consider the "half-civilized" Chinese, who "put a small iron shoe on the feet of their female infants, in order that they may be clumped up in a small space. True civilization presents no such gross interference with the course of nature."[25]

Fukuzawa translated these passages with his usual verve. Evil passions are rendered as *jōyoku* and the higher moral qualities of our nature as *reigi no michi*, terms immediately comprehensible to readers educated in the teachings of Confucius. But Fukuzawa balked at Burton's statement that civilization is merely "as natural" as barbarism. With the examples of head-boarding and foot-binding before him, he felt civilization was somehow more natural. So he dropped the "as natural" and wrote: "Of the things that transpire in civilized society, there is *not one* that does not come from nature *(tennen)* . . . Civilized society is the ultimate expression of what humans receive from heaven *(jinsei tenpin no shisei)*." Of the primitive age, however, he was only willing to say that *"most* of their customs come from nature *(shizen)*." *Tennen* and *shizen* both mean nature, but *tennen*, with the ideograph for *ten* (heaven), is a "better" nature. Similarly, *tenpin* can mean simply "natural endowment," or, depending on the context, it can carry the overtones of a gift from heaven. In his writings, Fukuzawa was generally, though not completely, consistent in using everyday terms *(shizen, ninjō, jōcho,* and so on) for man's lower nature and ideal terms (such as *tennen, tensei,* and *tenpin)* for the higher.[26]

Burton, following his Scottish predecessors, made two further points about civilization. The first is that civilized nations can discover their own distant past in the condition of present-day barbarous states. He compared, for example, the "despotic tyrants" who pillage the rich in contemporary Oriental nations with the feudal barons of medieval Europe who robbed Jews of their wealth.[27] He assumed that robbing the weak is normal behavior for rulers in a barbarous age, whether that age is in Europe's past or the Middle East's present. Similarly, when writing of the benefits of industry and civilization, Burton generalized: "If we wish to see the condition in which we would have been without these improvements, we can do so by examining the state of savage nations *(sōmai iteki no fūzoku)*, as it will be found described in books of travels."[28]

A second point is that progress is open-ended. In contrast to the geography texts, which seemed to present the "civilized and enlightened" West as a satisfactory culmination of history, Burton insisted that even those countries that represented the highest level of civilization were

imperfect at present but would improve in the future. An obvious failing of civilization was "the dreadful scourge of war." Nations today
"are still very nearly in the same position as individuals used to be" in
the dark ages of barbarism in that they attempt to settle their differences by strife. But progress has been made: "A system called the law of
nations . . . has been devised; and though there be no authority compelling nations to submit to it, yet it has some influence over them, since
they make enemies by infringing or overlooking it." Europe, for all of
its vaunted civilization, "is still apt at any moment to be overrun with
armies, and to be occupied in the barbarous pursuit of war." But there
is a remedy for such ills "in the progress of civilisation itself." Already
civilization has softened the horrors of war:

> The Red Indian of America only thinks how he can inflict the
> most dreadful misery on his enemies and all who are dear to them.
> He steals on a village at night, and murders all the women
> and children: if he is told that this is cowardly and brutal, he
> cannot understand how anyone could hesitate to take such an
> opportunity of indulging in revenge. In civilised warfare, it is
> deemed infamous to slay women and children, or any defenceless
> persons.[29]

As free trade and prosperity advance, he further asserted, nations will
become dependent on each other's goodwill, and "we may hope to see
war die away, and peace become in the end uninterrupted."[30]

Fukuzawa's translation of these passages is free but close to the original. He made only one significant change: instead of saying that the law
of nations "had some influence," he wrote, "there are none who do not
obey it."[31] Wanting Japan to take Europe as a model, he now and then
improved on the reality.

Government

Just as society existed from the earliest age of man, so had laws and
some form of rule. The most primitive peoples on earth, the Bushmen
of South Africa and the natives of Australia, Burton wrote, have among
them men of influence. Even the outcasts of society, "bands of robbers,
thieves, vagrants and the like," generally "have a kind of government

of their own." Italian banditti have chiefs, English highwaymen have commanders, and gypsies have their kings. Burton quoted with approval a didactic verse by Sir Walter Scott:

> Trust me, each state must have its policies,
> Kingdoms have edicts—cities have their charters;
> Even the wild outlaw in his forest walk
> keeps yet some touch of civil discipline;
> For, not since Adam wore his verdant apron,
> Hath man with man in social union dwelt,
> But laws were made to draw that union closer.[32]

Fukuzawa omitted the poem from his translation. He may not have understood Adam's "verdant apron," which to the Western reader suggests the knowledge of sin and the human condition in post-Edenic society. But he understood and accepted Burton's basic contention that some kind of law and rule was a part of human existence from the earliest times imaginable.

An early form of government was patriarchy. Burton cited historical passages from the Bible to demonstrate the early prevalence of this form of government in which "the heads of families" were "at the same time the chief magistrates or kings of small nations." He continued with examples from recent history:

> The Highlanders [of Scotland] were a set of clans or small nations . . . all who belonged to the same clan, and bore the same name, considered themselves as members of one family, and the head or chief was regarded as a parent. The Red Indians of America pay a filial duty to their chiefs: their only notion of government is that of a family with a patriarch ruling over it. Hence the Indians living in the United States call the president their Great Father. The Indians of Canada called the kings of Britain their Great Father, and on Queen Victoria's accession they were greatly puzzled, as they were not accustomed to give the title of ruler to a woman.[33]

In his translation of this passage, Fukuzawa deleted the Highlanders but kept the Indians and the Great Father. He often cut dull, irrelevant, or redundant materials, but never an amusing anecdote.

For most of human history, government was harsh, reflecting
the low level of civilization. The strong did as they pleased with the
weak.

> A Turkish pacha, were he offended by a slave, might cut him down
> at once with his sabre: a hundred and fifty years ago, a Highland
> chief might have done the same . . . In the dark ages, a cruel feudal
> lord of Germany, returning from the chase, caused one of his vas-
> sals to be slain and ripped up, that he might keep his feet warm in
> the reeking carcass: but if the greatest lord in England, on a cold
> day, were to seize a peasant's coat without his consent, he would be
> liable to be punished.[34]

After patriarchs, chiefs, and feudal lords, came kings. "Monarchy
generally takes its rise in simple chiefship, and such is its history in
most European countries."[35] At first, the territories ruled by kings were
small, but they were gradually expanded, usually by conquest. Burton
described the growth of Britain, France, Spain, Russia, and Prussia, and
argued: "The union of nations into large states is a great advantage.
It produces peace, and uniformity of laws, and of customs." If these
countries were still divided, they would be like Italy.[36] Once large kingdoms had been established, they evolved, variously, into the contemporary forms of European governments—mostly constitutional monarchies and republics. Fukuzawa's translation of these passages, too, was
straightforward.

Civilization as the Base of Government

Despite his richly detailed chapters on the subject, Burton viewed government almost as an epiphenomenon; what really mattered was civilization. He wrote:

> A totally unenlightened *(muchi mōmai)* community, like the people
> of Persia, can only have a despot over them . . . A people, on
> the contrary, enlightened and moral as most Europeans nations
> are, demands that its government be enlightened and moral also;
> and the government must be so, in order to secure public appro-
> bation.[37]

To Burton, Russia was almost as backward as Persia in its combination of an unenlightened people and despotism. But to make the point that even in unenlightened states popular opinion imposed limits on despots, he wrote:

> The emperor of Russia is the most powerful despot in the world, and his people reverence him more as a god *(kami no gotoshi)* than a man; yet they have peculiar customs and superstitions with which he could not meddle with safety, and more than one of his predecessors fell a victim to his plans for the improvement of the Russian people.[38]

Public opinion also matters in another regard: whatever the form of government may be, if it enjoys "the good-will and support of a large majority of the people," it will treat the opposition with mildness. If it does not, for the sake of "self-preservation," it will respond harshly to all who assail it.

> Owing to this principle, Austria, under the near absolute government *(rikkun dokusai)* of the amiable emperor, Francis II, was practically more free than France under the Republic of 1848; the latter government having been formed in accordance with the wishes of only a small minority of the people, and being consequently conducted with great difficulty.[39]

British government, too, owed less to "its form than its confidence in the good sense of the people. It admits of great personal freedom . . . because it knows this freedom . . . will not be abused."[40]

Education is another vital component of civilization. Burton devoted a chapter to the subject, following in large measure the arguments of Adam Smith. Education is a public good. It curtails crime and diminishes poverty. The state is obligated to provide it and citizens are obligated to support it through taxes. Even the special expenses of higher education are a legitimate use for government monies. Some may object that government should not interfere in family matters, but in the case of education the interference is justified. In politics, education makes people aware of their rights and of their responsibility toward government. "As morality and intelligence advance in a state," as civilization advances, "there is evidently a tendency to limit monarchical and extend representative authority."[41] While Burton had mixed feelings about the government of the United States, he had no doubts about its system of public education.

> It is above all things necessary, for a country under a system more or less democratic, that the people should be well educated; because they cannot otherwise be expected to perform their political duties in a proper manner. We find that in America, education has taken the form of a political necessity.[42]

Fukuzawa translated this chapter in its entirety. In 1868, as his many letters on the subject attest, he felt education to be Japan's highest priority.

Burton's Politics

Burton was a "liberal" in the nineteenth-century sense of the term, but less so than earlier Scottish writers. John Millar, as noted earlier, saw society as an intricate machine that could not easily be tinkered with, and in which sudden changes were likely to produce bad results. But for all of that, Millar was an ardent Whig, who acclaimed the Glorious Revolution of 1688, criticized many institutions of his own day, and sympathized with the early phases of the French Revolution. Burton, in contrast, lived in an age when laissez-faire liberalism was under attack by socialists. He saw himself as a defender of its truth, and his criticism of revolutionary change was, consequently, stronger than that of Millar. His politics merit a careful examination since they may have influenced Fukuzawa.

As mentioned earlier, at the beginning of *Political Economy*, the publishers told the readers that they lived in an age in which "the very foundations of civil society are attempted to be undermined." Burton saw eye to eye with his publishers. In a chapter titled "Objections to the Competitive System Considered" he spelled out his basic philosophy: "the competitive system" rose *"spontaneously"* and "is thus proved to have its basis in the mental constitution of man." It has "existed since the origin of human society"; it needed no law "to make it begin and . . . in every country and in every age it has been understood and trusted." He then contrasted this true view of a competitive human nature with the "theoretic" or "visionary" schemes based on "associative systems":

> The spectacle of a complete associative system, in which all individuality is lost; in which husbands and wives abandon their rights; in which children are brought up without knowing their parents; and all live amicably on a common stock, has never been realised. And it may be fairly presumed, that a system so flagrantly in violation of the first principles of the human constitution could not subsist beyond a very short period of time. The idle and evil disposed would live on the gains of the industrious; the crafty would overreach the unsuspicious.[43]

Burton concluded the chapter by arguing that we must not overturn "the structure of society for the purpose of trying new and visionary schemes which may do incalculable mischief before their fallacy be detected."[44]

Curiously, this chapter on objections to the competitive system was the only one of the fourteen chapters on social economy that Fukuzawa did not translate. It is not that he disagreed with Burton's argument; he translated without modifications the criticisms of visionary schemes that appeared in Burton's other chapters. Rather, we might conjecture, he felt no need to devote an entire chapter to such mistaken views, no need to confuse his Japanese readers by admitting that such views existed and had adherents in the West.

The French and British Systems

Because of his antipathy for theoretic schemes, Burton did not like revolutions. His basic outlook was that "sudden transitions from a despotic centralised government to one of a democratic character are not likely to be happy in their results." He was sufficiently flexible to make exceptions for the Glorious Revolution of 1688 and the American Revolution. In the Glorious Revolution, James II was at fault since he had "violated the laws of the country" and disrupted British institutions. In the case of America, Burton made a similar analysis, stressing the continuity of representative government.

The establishment of a republic in the British colonies of America is no exception to the rule; for these colonies had been accustomed to conduct their own affairs under representatives of the English sovereign, and had to make little change in the fabric of their government when they set up a Congress and President.

In America, the people naturally look back to their revolution with pride and self-congratulation, as it has unquestionably been to them the source of many blessings. Nevertheless, all the more respectable men concerned in these affairs would rather have avoided them if it had been possible.[45]

Such judgments were based on the general proposition that true progress in a civilization is always the result of slow changes in existing institutions. Even the customs of "barbarous times," if "fostered and improved," may "become the boasts of modern civilisation" (bunmei kaika no ichi daijo). In Britain, such improvements were exemplified by a host of institutions, such as the constitutional protections of British law, municipalities, the coroner's inquest, habeas corpus, trial by jury, the money power of the House of Commons, justice-of-the-peace tribunals, and town councils. These, he opined, are the "nurseries" of good government. They provide the "training in the conduct of public affairs . . . necessary . . . in order that any democratic kind of government . . . be well managed." They serve "the wants of civilisation" far better than "the ingenious systems prepared by scholars" (gakusha no kōron ni shitaigaite hō o tsukuru yori).[46]

In contrast to the wisdom of British institutions, Burton found France lacking on every count.[47] The French, he wrote, have no such nurseries of good government, "not even so simple an expedient as habeas corpus." They attempt to leap ahead by revolution, and inevitably fail:

> The French have repeatedly passed laws in favour of freedom, liberty, and equality, and yet every one who gets the upper hand there becomes a tyrant (bōkun): there seems to be no other way of preserving order. The new laws made for freedom are not identified with the constant habits and everyday customs of the people (kokumin no shūzoku ni tekisezushite), and thus they are easily upset.[48]

What was wrong with France's revolutions is the common failing of all "associative systems." They are based on the theoretic constructs of philosophers, not on actual institutions. They reflect what philosophers want man to be and not what he is. They are artificial and contrary to nature.

In their economic life, as well, the French came up short. When Napoleon invaded Russia in 1812, his army had "a vast organization of cattle-drivers, butchers, millers, bakers, and cooks," and he "exercised his own great genius in organising them." But it was to no avail since provisions were in short supply and "many thousands died of starvation." Even hanging and shooting those who were responsible did not remedy the problem. Burton's explanation was that human artifice was no substitute for the natural workings of the market.[49]

Another instance of an unnatural economic "folly" cited by Burton took place in Paris after the revolution of 1848. The French government employed 1,500 tailors to produce a certain number of uniforms for the army. In line with its egalitarian philosophy, rather than pay each tailor individually for work done, the government promised an equal division of the total payment among all of the 1,500 workers.

> But they looked much disconcerted when the work was done, and the money divided among them, for it came to less than the worst worker among them would have got in ordinary employment. They had, in fact, been lazy at the work, and the reason was very obvious. If any one of them exerted himself, he got no benefit by his exertion, unless the whole 1500 exerted themselves precisely to the same extent.[50]

Burton concluded that there are matters "which it is mischievous for a government to interfere with."[51]

In contrast to French attempts to contravene the natural laws of economics, Burton offered London and the natural workings of its market:

> It contains upwards of two millions of inhabitants. These are calculated to consume daily 300 bullocks, 2126 sheep, 700 lambs, and a like number of calves and pigs; bread amounting to 175350

quartern-loaves; 62 hundredweights of cheese, and 27534 gallons of milk. If for any one day this supply were to fall short by a half, or even a third, the suffering and confusion would be terrible: yet such a thing never happens, and the ordinary citizen lives with a feeling of security, as if it never would or could happen. When he rises at eight o'clock, he may have sent to him, or he may buy a few doors off, the fresh rolls which have been carefully prepared by men who have risen at four to knead them and place them in the oven. The meal they are made with has been brought from a miller, whose grain has perhaps been grown partly in England, partly in Scotland, and some of it on the Ohio, on the Black Sea, and on the Baltic: the sugar, which he can obtain as easily . . . has been grown and manufactured by black men of the East or of the West, within the tropics; the tea is planted for him ten thousand miles away, and tended, plucked, and sorted for his use in the interior of a vast, unknown empire, by a race of men whose appearance would be a show to him.[52]

Burton commented: "It will at once be pretty apparent that no human ingenuity could arrange and keep regularly going so complicated a machine." While translating this passage in its entirety, Fukuzawa must have thought of the teeming market economy of Edo.

Burton summed up his long chapter on "The Nature of Political Economy" with the following statement:

From these few examples, it is perceived that political economy is not an artificial system *(jin'i no hō)*, but an explanation of the operation of certain natural laws *(onozukara yo ni okonawaruru tennen no hōsoku)*. In explaining this system, the teacher is not more infallible than the teacher of geology or medicine. It is clear, however, that the more we study and observe, the nearer we get at the truth . . . In this, as in all other matters, it will be found that knowledge is far better than ignorance.[53]

Fukuzawa and Western Learning

In translating Burton, Fukuzawa was telling his readers, "This is what Westerners think." He called the book *Conditions in the West* and stated that it depicted the "beams, foundation, roof, and walls" that "Western nations have in common." But Fukuzawa was also saying, "This is what is true." With Japan as his yardstick, he measured Burton's propositions about human nature and human institutions and discovered that by and large they fit. That he approved is borne out by his repeated use of ideas from *Political Economy* in his later writings.

In 1868, his Keiō School moved to its new campus at Mita. Fukuzawa delivered an inaugural speech in which he reaffirmed his vision of the truth of Western learning and described the daunting task that lay before his faculty and students:

> What sets Western learning apart from all other learning is that it originates in nature, elucidates nature's laws *(butsuri)*, teaches the way of morality *(jindō)*, and orders the relations between individuals and society. It is truth with no trace of falsehood, containing all knowledge, large and small. Since we must study Western learning to fulfill ourselves as human beings, should it not be called the study of heaven's truth *(tenshin no gaku)?* We scholars of Western learning have studied this learning for years but have barely scratched its surface. We cannot help but constantly sigh when confronted by the vastness of its manifold fields. This truly must be called a great undertaking.[54]

The great undertaking remained Fukuzawa's central concern during the decade that followed. His first major original work was *An Encouragement of Learning (Gakumon no susume)*. The content of the second, *Outline of Theories of Civilization (Bunmeiron no gairyaku)*, was equally an encouragement of learning.

~ 4

Invention, the Engine of Progress

By his admirable contrivances, it [the steam engine] has become a thing stupendous alike for its force and its flexibility, for the prodigious power which it can exert, and the ease and precision and ductility with which it can be varied, distributed, and applied. The trunk of an elephant that can pick up a pin or rend an oak, is as nothing to it. It can engrave a seal, and crush masses of obdurate metal like wax before it; draw out, without breaking, a thread as fine as gossamer, and lift a ship of war like a bauble in the air. It can embroider muslin, and forge anchors; cut steel into ribbons, and impel loaded vessels against the fury of the winds and waves.

—Lord Francis Jeffrey, 1763–1850

Technology in Fukuzawa's Early Thought

For the Japanese after 1853, military technology was the immediately comprehensible and visible face of Western civilization. The Tokugawa bakufu and daimyo alike vied to purchase rifles, cannon, and steamships. When Fukuzawa left his domain in 1855, it was to study Dutch and Western gunnery. While studying in Osaka he copied and translated a Western work on fortifications. Later, in 1869 and 1870, to establish his livelihood, he translated other treatises on military topics.

Fukuzawa's earliest writing on technology may have been in passages of the *Fukuda Sakutarō hikki*, the report of the 1862 bakufu mission to Europe. The report bears the name of a higher official, but was actually written by lower-ranking interpreters who accompanied the mission. Fukuzawa was one of several; we do not know how the responsibility was divided among them.[1] The few sections that touch on technology are bland and descriptive. They note that railway and telegraph companies are private, not governmental, and that they were established only

Fukuzawa in Europe, 1862. At age twenty-seven, Fukuzawa (far right) was an
interpreter with the 1862 bakufu mission to Europe. Standing next to Fukuzawa
is Seki Shinpachi, another interpreter, and seated at the center wearing two
swords is Ono Tomogorō, the head of the mission.

in recent decades. They describe systems and costs, but say little about
how the new technology worked, though the entry on gas lamps states
that the gas is produced from burning coal and is sent through pipes to
the lamps.

Fukuzawa's travels in Europe certainly influenced his decision to begin his first major writing project, *Conditions in the West.* An 1864 draft
of the first part of that work contains entries on the steam engine, the
telegraph, and gas lamps. In comparison to entries on the same topics in the 1862 report, they are greatly improved: the writing style is
clearer and more colorful, and the draft includes new information from
books Fukuzawa had read after returning to Japan. The telegraph, he
wrote, sends messages through copper wires by electrical energy. It
links London to India, St. Petersburg to Siberia, "covering immense
distances in an instant." Trains are propelled by the power of steam;
they run quickly over iron rails on a flat roadbed. To build a line between Marseilles and Paris required cutting through mountains and

bridging valleys. The railroad is "a necessity for mobilizing troops in time of war," and, he exclaimed, is "truly like a ship of the land." His description of gas lamps was little changed from the earlier report, though with Edo in mind, he added, "In the cities of Europe today, where gas plants exist, no one carries a lantern on the streets at night."[2]

The first volume of *Conditions in the West*, which I call *Conditions I*, was published in 1866. The opening chapter presented twenty-four short sketches of the artifacts and institutions of civilization that had impressed Fukuzawa during his 1862 visit to Europe and about which he had read further after returning to Japan. To enumerate, five of the sketches treat institutions of learning: schools, newspapers, libraries, museums, and exhibitions. Seven touch on political institutions, or, at least, institutions that had close government connections: forms of government, tax laws, national debts, paper money, foreign relations, military systems, and commercial companies. Another six treat institutions established to meet the special needs of society's unfortunates: poorhouses, hospitals, and schools or asylums for the mentally deficient, insane, blind, deaf and dumb. To Fukuzawa, the existence of these institutions was evidence that "civilization" brought not only wealth and power, but also a better understanding of human nature and higher moral standards. He would reiterate this point nine years later in *Outline of Theories of Civilization*.

> Having investigated the nature and behavior *(seishitsu to hataraki)* of human beings, they [Western scholars] have gradually come to understand the laws *(teisoku)* of human nature and are close to devising systems to manage it. To give several examples of their progress: Their laws are fine-grained and few persons are unjustly condemned. Commercial laws are clear and convenient . . . Tax laws are skillfully devised so that few lose their property. The laws of warfare are detailed, and though they deal with the art of killing, the result is that fewer die. International law is loose and easily circumvented, yet it somewhat reduces the likelihood of war . . . All of these increasingly detailed and extensive regulations are conducive to a better moral order *(daitoku no koto)*.[3]

In 1897, in the introduction to the first edition of his *Collected Works*, he recollected his amazement on first visiting Europe:

Hospitals, poorhouses, schools for the blind and the deaf, insane asylums, museums and expositions, were all new to our eyes, and as we learned of their origins and operations, we became entranced. Our feelings were just like those of Koreans who come to Japan today and are astonished by everything they see and hear. But while most Koreans just go home astonished, we felt not only astonishment but also envy, and the desire arose within us to establish such institutions in Japan.[4]

The last five sketches in *Conditions I* treat five technologies: the steam engine, the locomotive, the steamship, the telegraph, and gas lamps. In comparison to the 1864 draft, the sketches are more detailed and reflect a deeper understanding. Because Fukuzawa had read more, he could explain the technologies better. When water boils and turns into steam, he wrote, it expands to a volume 1,700 times greater, and the steam, contained in cylinders, drives the engine. He also addressed the history of each technology. "In early times the West was no different from Japan or China in using human labor for production. In 1720, a German named Leupold theorized that steam could be substituted for human labor, and then, between 1769 and 1785, an Englishman, Watt, succeeded in making a steam engine." There followed descriptions of Watt's further efforts and innovations, and of the steam engine's use in manufacturing. As a result, at present, "artisans need attend only to the workings of the machine, without using the power of their hands and feet, and one person can do the work of one hundred."[5]

Fukuzawa's sketch of locomotives also related the circumstances of its invention. In 1784, the Englishman William Murdock constructed the first locomotive, though it was "little more than a toy." After that, twenty years passed without progress until, in 1802, Richard Trethefik made a further advance in engine design, but it still "lacked practical applications." In 1813, George Stephenson succeeded in building a locomotive that could be used to haul coal. Finally, in 1825, Stephenson built tracks between Stockton and Darlington, towns in northern England, and established the world's first railroad. This achievement was quickly imitated and railroads were built throughout Europe and America.[6]

By giving these historical details, Fukuzawa was telling his compatriots that technological innovation was not easy and often took years to attain, but once achieved, spread rapidly. He also noted that almost seventy years had elapsed between the electrical experiments of the Frenchman Lesage and Morse's successful completion of the world's first telegraph line between Washington and Baltimore in 1844. After that, progress was fast: a submarine cable was laid between Dover and the French coast by 1851, and another across the Atlantic by 1858.

The sketches vividly describe the social consequences of the new technologies.

> In Western countries telegraph lines spread out in all directions across land and seas just like a spider's web. They exchange news and communicate urgent messages even to persons thousands of miles distant . . . Westerners do not exaggerate when they say that the invention of the telegraph has made the world smaller.[7]

As for the railroad, it facilitated travel between city and countryside, and goods were shipped from where they were plentiful to where they were scarce, lessening differences of price. People traveled about with greater ease: "Westerners say that the people of their countries no longer hear flimsy excuses such as 'I was traveling when I heard of the illness of my mother, father, wife, or child, and because of the distance was unable to return before they died.'"[8]

Learning and Technology

Fukuzawa's interest in the history of invention and scientific discovery is also evident in one other sketch in *Conditions I*, titled "Learning and Technology" *(Bungaku gijutsu)*. Wanting to give his readers a more general overview of the long centuries it had taken Europe to develop science and the new technologies, Fukuzawa translated materials from three chapters in Alexander Fraser Tytler's *Elements of General History.*[9] The chapters, which supplement the other predominantly political chapters, treat science, literature, historiography, music, and art. Fukuzawa extracted the materials on science and presented them in a simplified form.

The first of the three was titled "A View of the Progress of Literature and Science in Europe, from the Revival of Letters down to the end of the Fifteenth Century." It began:

The first restorers of learning in Europe were the Arabians, who, in the course of their Asiatic conquests, becoming acquainted with some of the ancient Greek authors, discovered and justly appreciated the knowledge and improvement to be derived from them. The caliphs procured from the eastern emperors copies of the ancient manuscripts, and had them carefully translated into Arabic, esteeming principally those which treated of mathematics, physic, and metaphysics. They disseminated their knowledge in the course of their conquests, and founded schools and colleges in all the countries which they subdued. The western kingdoms of Europe became first acquainted with the learning of the ancients through the medium of these Arabian translations.[10]

Fukuzawa drastically condensed the passage as follows (I translate back from the Japanese):

Once Greek learning declined, it was the Arabs who revived it. They worked especially in the fields of mathematics (*sokuryōgaku*, literally, "the study of measurements"), medicine, and physics/ metaphysics (*rigaku*). The development of learning and technology in European countries thereafter was entirely a gift from the Arabs.[11]

Next, Fukuzawa translated the larger part of the following Tytler passage:

In the middle of the thirteenth century appeared a distinguished genius, Roger Bacon, an English friar, whose comprehensive mind was filled with all the stores of ancient learning; who possessed a discriminating judgment to separate the precious ore from the dross, and a power of invention fitted to advance in every science which was the object of his study. He saw the insufficiency of the school philosophy, and first recommended the prosecution of knowledge by experiment and the observation of nature. He made discoveries of importance in astronomy, in optics, in chemistry and medicine, and mechanics. He reformed the calendar, discovered the construction of telescopic glasses, forgotten after his time, and revived by Galileo, and has left a plain intimation of his

88

knowledge of the composition of gunpowder. Yet this most superior genius believed in the possibility of discovering an elixir for the prolongation of life, in the transmutation of metals into gold, and in judicial astrology.[12]

Fukuzawa cut out the next seven paragraphs, which dealt with literature, yet included the following line: "But although poetry attained in these ages [the fifteenth century] a considerable degree of splendour, there was but little advancement in general literature and science." His translation reads (my retranslation): "From this time until the 1400s, learned men took pleasure in poetry and novels but few exerted themselves with studies of what is real *(jitsugaku)*."[13]

Fukuzawa continued his sketch with materials from a second chapter in Tytler titled "A View of the Progress of Science and Literature in Europe, from the End of the Fifteenth to the End of the Seventeenth Century." Following the text, Fukuzawa touched on the invention of printing, the dogmas of Aristotle and their relation to theology, the experimental science of Francis Bacon and Descartes, and the discoveries of Galileo.[14] He shielded his readers from the information that Galileo had been "rewarded by imprisonment, as a supporter of the Copernican heresy," skipped over descriptions of the discoveries of Kepler and Napier, but included Harvey's discovery of the circulation of blood and the entire account of the genius of Newton. Wielding his usual razor, he then cut out Locke, Spenser, Milton, Shakespeare, Dryden, Corneille, Racine, Molière, Machiavelli, a host of lesser literary figures, and the English historians.

A third chapter in Tytler was titled "A View of the Progress of Literature, Science, and Art, in Europe, from the Commencement of the Eighteenth Century to the Present Time." It was almost a catalog of modern poets, authors, dramatists, musicians, philosophers, and painters in England, Germany, and France. Fukuzawa skipped over all of these materials, but translated almost in its entirety the following list of "the many new and valuable discoveries and inventions."

Steam engines, steam-boats, steam and atmospheric railways, the electric telegraph, vaccination, printing of linen and cotton cloths, paper for rooms, figured silks and carpets, the spinning jenny, spinning frame, and power loom, stereotype printing, and lithography, musical type, electrotype, lighting conductors, life boats, safety lamps, telegraphs, gas lights, balloons, and a host of electrical, galvanic, pneumatic, optical, and astronomical instruments and apparatus.[15]

In writing this little sketch, Fukuzawa intended to provide a simple background history for science. Nothing need be said here of his excision of the arts. But we might note that similar cuts were made in the translations of other works whenever he encountered materials on the arts or literature. In translating the histories of Western nations for *Conditions in the West I* and *III*, he routinely eliminated descriptions of what he considered the "non-practical" aspects of their civilizations. Perhaps he felt that Japan had a rich literary tradition yet, despite this, had fallen behind in its progress toward civilization. Whatever the reasons, his analysis of Western civilization had no room for Greek drama or Shakespeare.

The Sociology of Invention

In 1868 Fukuzawa's attention shifted from technology and its history to the process of invention and its social setting. He looked at the circumstances of the most prominent inventors, at the ideas that encouraged invention, and at the laws that rewarded great achievements. What is so special about the West? he seemed to ask. Why is it that the transformative technologies of recent centuries have been developed in the West and not in Japan? He never made the comparison explicit but it was always in the back of his mind and the materials he presented may be seen as a response to it. His analysis of invention was presented as additional segments in the supplementary volume of *Conditions in the West*. It was interpolated into his translation of Burton's *Political Economy* and may have been stimulated by his reading of that work.

Writing of society as a competitive system, Burton defined the civilized state as one in which "a man in advancing himself, benefits his species."

Thus, great inventors who have obtained distinguished fame, and have often made large fortunes, have been signal benefactors to their species: such as Watt, Hargreaves, Arkwright, Stephenson, and others who have brought to perfection the steam-engine, the manufacturing machinery, and the railway system. Such, also, are the great authors and artists who have appeared from time to time: and not only those who are conspicuous and distinguished, but those who have humbly helped to carry out their projects, have benefited the rest of the world while seeking their own emolument and advancement.[16]

Fukuzawa translated the passage, deleting only the phrase "great authors and artists." This passage alone would have sufficed to convince his readers of the critical importance of invention. But Fukuzawa wanted to hammer the point home. So he decided to provide more detail about the lives of the greatest inventors and the social settings that had nourished and challenged them. He sandwiched into his translation of Burton short biographies of James Watt and George Stephenson. The biographies, which he found in the *New American Cyclopaedia*, were, as befit the spirit of the age, highly laudatory. In Fukuzawa's translation they became even more so.

Following the *Cyclopaedia* text, Fukuzawa began his account with the span of Watt's life from his birth in 1736 in Greenock to his death in 1819 in Heathfield. The *Cyclopaedia* entry states that Watt's father was "a merchant and builder . . . and for many years held important offices in the town; but the loss of his fortune and prostration of his faculties later in life occasioned his withdrawal from business." Fukuzawa changed this to "a rich shipbuilder, who in his later years became bankrupt," and deleted the "prostration of his faculties."[17] Fukuzawa included the information about the father's bankruptcy in order to explain why the father could not afford to give his son a systematic education. After describing Watt's sickliness as a child, the English text continued, "He early showed a great fondness for mathematics and mechanical contrivances, and at about the age of 14 he constructed for his own use an electrical machine." In the translation, the "great fondness" became "did research in" *(kenkyū shi)*. The *Cyclopaedia* entry then relates the well-known anecdote about Watt's aunt, who complained that Watt idly wasted his time by "watching a boiling tea kettle, taking off and replacing its lid, observing the exit of steam from the spout, holding a spoon . . . over the escaping jet, and counting the drops of water that condensed on it." Fukuzawa translated the anecdote in its entirety.

By the age of eighteen, the *Cyclopaedia* tells us, the studious Watt had "made considerable attainments in botany, chemistry, and mineralogy, [and] still more in natural philosophy." In the Japanese, Watt's "considerable attainments" became even more impressive: "Especially in natural philosophy, he arrived at its innermost secrets" *(koto ni kyūrigaku ni oite wa sono ōgi ni tasshi)*. Later Watt became a skilled instrument-maker, an artisan of sorts, with a workshop within the precincts of Glasgow University. A university student who became acquainted with Watt expressed "his surprise at finding in young Watt not merely an intelligent workman, but a philosopher also." In the Japanese translation, "philosopher" became "a great scholar of natural philosophy *(kyūrigaku no ichi daisensei)*." While in Glasgow, Watt "mastered German and Italian," and "though destitute of the perception of melody, he also so far perfected himself in the theory of music as to construct an organ of excellent quality." Fukuzawa deleted all mention of these polite accomplishments.

Fukuzawa next turned to Watt's development of the steam engine and the patents that protected his interests. As usual, Fukuzawa stressed the positive aspects of the story. He told his readers about the financial support given to Watt by John Roebuck in 1768 and Matthew Boulton in 1774, about the original five-year patent of 1769 and the twenty-five-year extension of the patent in 1775; he also mentioned that Watt received royalties throughout those years. But the *Cyclopaedia* also told of Roebuck's "mining speculations," which led to "his embarrassment and abandonment of the enterprise." Fukuzawa changed this to "afterwards Roebuck was busy with mining . . . and had no leisure in which to complete the steam engine." Fukuzawa also neglected to tell his readers that the twenty-five-year extension was granted "despite great opposition" in Parliament. He omitted, as well, any mention of Watt's long struggles against those who ignored his patents, and the "harassing anxieties of lawsuits" that "drew severely upon the capabilities of a naturally feeble constitution." But he did include Lord Jeffrey's poetic encomium on Watt's invention, which is given at the head of this chapter.

Fukuzawa wrapped up his biographical sketch with the statement that Watt "retired to his country estate *(den'en)* at Heathfield, where, in the company of scholarly friends, he spent his remaining years communing with nature *(fūgetsu o tanoshinde)*. Based as it is on information in *Cyclopaedia*, this is not a bad ending. Watt, along with such luminaries as Priestley and Darwin, was a member of the "Lunar Society," which held its monthly meetings on the night of the full moon. But the impression it gives is of a gentle country squire sitting back and enjoying the rewards of his earlier creativity. The *Cyclopaedia* entry, in contrast, suggests that he was active to the end of his life, carrying out scientific experiments, writing, and participating in academic societies.

Fukuzawa also translated the *Cyclopaedia* entry on George Stephenson (1781–1848), the inventor of the locomotive. Because Stephenson's life was the story of triumph over adversity, it needed less improvement in the telling. Even more than Watt, Stephenson had a deprived childhood. As a boy of nine he tended the neighbor's cows for two pence a day; at eighteen "he was still ignorant of reading, and even of the letters of the alphabet." Fukuzawa rendered the latter as "could not even read his own name." Only twice did Fukuzawa alter the original. Describing Stephenson's situation at the age of twenty-three, the English text relates:

> In 1802 he [Stephenson] was married, but became a widower within two years, and removed in 1805 with his infant son, Robert, to Killingworth colliery, where his little earnings were speedily absorbed by the demands which his father's poverty imposed upon him, and by the payment of a considerable sum to procure a substitute in the militia, for which he had been drawn.[18]

Fukuzawa transformed "demands . . . imposed upon him" into spontaneous acts of filial piety: "he often relieved the poverty of his parent" *(shibashiba fubo no konkyū o sukui)*, and omits entirely the fact that Stephenson bought his way out of military service.[19]

Later, after Stephenson perfected the locomotive, a railway line was opened between Liverpool and Manchester. The *Cyclopaedia* describes the event:

> At the ceremony of the opening of the road, Sept. 15, 1830, Mr. Huskisson, who was in attendance with many other distinguished public men, having been accidentally struck down and fatally in-

jured by this engine, was conveyed in it from Parkside to Eccles, a distance of 15 miles, at the then unprecedented rate of 36 miles an hour.[20]

Fukuzawa was loath to inform his audience of the lethal potential of so wondrous an invention as the steam locomotive. He made no mention of the hapless Mr. Huskisson, and simply stated that the train traveled thirty-six miles in one hour.

After inserting the two biographical sketches, Fukuzawa returned to his translation of Burton's *Political Economy*. The last three translated chapters dealt with property: its origin and nature, its protection, and the protection of its profits. Burton spoke of "the sense of property," which "seems to pervade all living beings as an instinct."

> The bird enjoys the property of its nest . . . The bows and arrows of the Indian are his property; if they were not, and if he were liable to give them up to the rest of his tribe, he would never undergo the trouble of making them. Thus, from the very beginning, the advantage of property is felt: it induces men to create what they would not otherwise create, and improves their condition.[21]

Among civilized men, property is yet more complicated. Burton distinguished between "heritable property" such as houses and lands, and "movable property" such as money, furniture, pictures, or shares of stock. He then added:

> There are still more nice and complicated kinds of property than even these. Such, for instance, are patents and copyrights. We shall see presently that the law protects property, that people may be induced to make it by their industry. Inventions are of great benefit to the human race; and that people may have an inducement to become inventors, the law of patent gives them the exclusive use of the invention for a certain time. A gentleman invented a method of making cloth waterproof. He obtained a patent, by which he enjoyed for a certain time the sole privilege of making cloth waterproof by the invention he had discovered: this was said to be his property. It was a monopoly. Monopolies are profitable to those who possess them, and are a loss to the public; but then

the inventor does more than pay for the loss by his valuable invention. Authors who write books, and artists who make designs, have
a property of the same kind, called copyright.[22]

Fukuzawa unerringly zeroed in on the two critical points in this passage: the theoretical justification for the special treatment of intellectual property, and the laws required to guarantee that inventors and authors would receive such treatment. To reinforce these points, he once
again interpolated outside materials into his translation.

His source for the first interpolation, a justification of intellectual
property, was a section titled "The Different Forms of Human Industry" in Francis Wayland's *The Elements of Political Economy*.[23] Having already done justice to the role of inventors in his biographical sketches,
Fukuzawa skipped Wayland's first subsection, which discussed "discovery" and "invention" and mentioned such figures as Isaac Newton,
Benjamin Franklin, Humphrey Davy, and Robert Fulton. He went directly to the next subsection, "Of the Different Products of the Various
Forms of Industry."

This subsection was more theoretical. Wayland first differentiated
between physical labor that makes "material products" and mental labor that creates "immaterial products." Material products are subject
to the "ordinary rules of supply and demand, cost and labor," but the
products of mental labor are not. The chief characteristic of immaterial
products—he also calls them "intellectual products"—is that they "may
require the exercise of the most unusual talent, and may demand both
protracted and expensive labor," but once discovered or invented, they
may be reproduced quite simply "by men of the most ordinary talent."
"Hence, he who first creates knowledge, has no means of monopoliz-
ing it; nor can the exchangeable value be sustained."[24]

Yet the products of mental labor are just as necessary to the well-
being of a community as those of physical labor, for without them "we
should all be savages." Therefore, Wayland continued, civil society
"has frequently devised means by which some remuneration may be
reaped from the exercise of this kind of industry. Such are the laws of
copy, and of patent right." In making this argument, Wayland was not
belittling the contribution of physical labor. He wrote: "A society composed solely of philosophers, or inventors, or professional men, would
never grow rich, but must . . . of necessity starve." His vision of society,

which Fukuzawa eloquently translated, was of different classes of la-
borers joined in a "harmonious co-operation" to "increase production,
and thus add to the conveniences and happiness of man."[25]

In a second interpolation, Fukuzawa turned from economic theory
to the laws protecting those who make immaterial products. For this he
drew on the entries on patents and copyrights in the *New American
Cyclopaedia* and the entry on patents in *Brande's Dictionary of Science, Literature and Art*.[26] The entries are long and legalistic, slow going even
for a native English speaker. Fukuzawa, aiming at succinctness and
readability, cut them to the bare bones.

The *Cyclopaedia* entry on "PATENTS, Law of:" stated that patents are
unique to Europe and the United States, and that even there, they are
comparatively recent. It further stated that the theory of patents rests
not on common law or natural rights, but resembles, rather, the laws of
contract: "the public agreeing, in consideration of the inventor telling
all about his invention instead of keeping it a secret, that what is new
and useful shall become his vested right and property for a certain
time." Fukuzawa translated most of this as well as the following sen-
tence, a pithier restatement of Wayland's argument: "The purpose of
the patent law is to encourage invention for the public good, by the
stimulus of the large rewards which a monopoly of any useful instru-
ment must yield."[27]

Fukuzawa then skipped over several paragraphs treating such details
as the status of patents in law, who may apply for a patent, and "what
may be the subject of patent," and turned to the practical question of
"how letters patent may be obtained." He described the process. An application had to be sent to the commissioner with drawings attached. A
model had to be furnished whenever that is "the best way of illustrating
the specification, a working model being preferable." The *Cyclopaedia*
entry also described the patent office in which "there is a careful and
well devised arrangement of all the models gathered since the destruc-
tion of the former patent building on Dec. 15, 1836."[28] Fukuzawa, in
fact, had visited the patent office in Washington, D.C., on May 30,
1867, during his second trip to the United States.[29] Apparently his
fancy was taken by the rooms that were filled with shelf upon shelf of
tiny working models of the most recent machinery of civilization. So
when he translated the sentence about models, he added details based
on his own experience:

In this office were displayed all kinds of instruments and ma-
chines, writing implements and weapons, clothing and accessories,
textiles and designs, etc.—thousands and tens of thousands of the
drawings and models of those who had applied for patents over
the years.[30]

Fukuzawa completed his description of the American system with a
short passage on the cost and duration of patents, caveats that apply,
and the penalties for claiming a patent where none existed. He then
turned to *Brande's Dictionary* for a quick look at the patent system in
England. Again, he described how an inventor filed a specification, the
cost of the patent, and the cost of additional extensions. He ended his
account of the English system with the information: "The number of
patents now annually sealed is said to be about 2,000; of which not
above 200 on the average continue beyond the first seven years."[31]

For copyrights, Fukuzawa relied solely on the *Cyclopaedia*. The entry
began by noting that property originally had meant "material things,"
and that it took years for "modern society" to recognize "intellectual
property" as a new object of law. Fukuzawa felt this was particularly
relevant to Japan, where ideas were not viewed as property. Most of
the rest of his translation dealt with the duration of copyrights in various countries: England, forty-two years or the lifetime of the author;
the United States, twenty-eight years and a renewal of fourteen more;
France and Belgium, the author's lifetime plus twenty years; Bavaria,
Würtemburg, and the German confederation, the lifetime plus thirty
years; and Russia, the lifetime plus twenty-five years. The details were
important: here, as in other parts of *Conditions*, Fukuzawa was providing a guide for use by future lawmakers in Japan. His account of
copyrights ended with a mention of Parliament's attempt to afford
protection for British authors by establishing international copyright
agreements. Some nations had assented, but in the United States the
Senate had defeated the measure.[32]

Given Fukuzawa's nearly total lack of interest in Western prose, poetry, music, or art, and the deletions he made when these subjects appeared in his English sources, one might ask why he bothered with
copyrights at all. It was partly because he placed a high value on practical subjects such as history, politics, and economics; they deserved protection. It was partly because he wished to protect his own interests. He

was highly indignant when he learned that pirated editions of *Conditions I* were being sold in western Japan, and sent off a stream of complaints to his agent in Osaka.

There was a certain innocence in his unvoiced assumption that the piracy of works by foreign authors, of which he was Japan's most accomplished practitioner, and domestic piracy, of which he was the most prominent victim, were entirely different matters. Indeed, he may not even have been aware of the contradiction. Had he been asked about his inconsistency, he might have replied, drawing on both Wayland and the *Cyclopaedia* entry, that international copyrights are a matter of law, not nature, and that in the absence of laws, no wrong is involved. Still, the absence of copyright laws in Japan before 1869 did not in the least deter him from protesting the domestic piracy of his works.

Weighing the Record

How, then, are we to judge Fukuzawa's detailed analysis of invention? Did he merely piece together materials he happened to have at hand? Or did he exhibit an extraordinary insight into the workings of a critical area in modern Western society?

In support of a pieced-together approach, we note that Burton's *Political Economy* provided Fukuzawa with a conceptual framework for his treatment of invention. He had demonstrated considerable foresight in buying histories, geographies, gazetteers, works on political economy, and other reference works, including the *New American Cyclopaedia* and *Brande's Dictionary*, during his trips abroad. When he came across Watt and Stephenson in *Political Economy*, he promptly looked them up in the *Cyclopaedia*, translated appropriate passages, and put them in his text. He found entries on patents and copyrights in the same source. His inclusion of the passage on intellectual property from Wayland's *Elements of Political Economy* was an indirect consequence of the instruction he gave at his school: he taught a class on Wayland in 1868. He may have begun reading *Elements of Political Economy* during the second half of 1867 while writing the supplementary volume of *Conditions*. The similarity between Wayland and Burton on the subject of intellectual property must have caught his eye; it was but a small step to put in the pertinent passage from Wayland. In short, the piecing together of a coherent view of invention may be viewed as a simple additive process.

I am more inclined, however, to see Fukuzawa's inquiry into the wellsprings of invention as extraordinarily insightful. He had been studying English for less than a decade; he had just begun serious translations of Western history only two or three years before writing the supplementary volume of *Conditions*. Japan had no tradition of scholarship on Western society or history; the few writings by scholars of Dutch Studies were next to useless for his purposes. For his intellectual base, he had to appropriate the West's grasp of its own history. In so doing, he immediately perceived that technologies were a dynamic new element in recent Western history and that their source lay in the process of invention. He approached invention as a social process and analyzed it in terms of multiple variables.

If any new institution is to be accepted, it must be accompanied by a rationale that justifies its place in the scheme of things. For private property in a competitive system and the need to protect it by law, Fukuzawa relied on Burton's *Political Economy*. For intellectual property and the need to grant noncompetitive monopolies to those who create it, he used both Burton and Wayland. For the legal institutions that protect such monopolies and reward inventors, he turned to *Cyclopaedia* and *Brande's Dictionary*. In presenting these materials, Fukuzawa was, in effect, explaining to his readers why inventors such as Watt and Stephenson had not appeared in Japan.

But he may also have been suggesting that Japan's future was not necessarily bleak. The human dimension of his brief biographies told of poverty and hardship, obstacles overcome, hard work, and inspiration that led eventually to fortune and fame. As he put together his materials, Fukuzawa must have thought that the Japanese, too, were willing to work hard and sacrifice in pursuit of a goal. If they could only change their way of thinking and be assured of a few legal protections, they, too, would become capable of great works of invention. He wrote not to lament Japan's failings but to spell out and encourage the changes he felt necessary. And he arrived at this understanding in an age when some scholars were still talking "Eastern ethics and Western technology."

As far as I have been able to ascertain, no other thinker in a non-Western land arrived at a comparable analysis during the nineteenth century. Several wrote of patents, though not in comparable detail, but none wrote of the peculiar nature of intellectual property or of the social setting of invention. It is easier to describe the steps by which Fukuzawa put together his analysis than to explain why no one else did so. Other countries were closer to Europe, had longer histories of contact, and more people who spoke European languages. Other countries also had institutions comparable to the Gaikokugata (Tokugawa foreign ministry). Why did they not produce comparable thinkers? At this point, Fukuzawa's accomplishment seems to stand alone.

~ 5

An Outline of Theories of Civilization

After Perry arrived and the Tokugawa government signed treaties with the foreign powers, the people observed the government's dispositions and learned for the first time how stupid and weak they were. Also, as they made contact with foreigners, listened to their words, and read Western books and translations, their knowledge widened ever more, and they came to realize that even a government of demons and gods (*kishin*) could be overthrown by human efforts. It was as if the deaf and blind had suddenly opened their ears and eyes, and for the first time realized that they could hear sounds and see colors . . . Meeting with Westerners for the first time in their history, it was as if the Japanese had emerged from the dark silence of deepest night into the clamorous brawl of full daylight. Everything they saw was strange, and nothing fit their preconceptions.

—Fukuzawa Yukichi, 1875

AN OUTLINE OF THEORIES OF CIVILIZATION (*Bunmeiron no gairyaku*), published in 1875, represents the culmination of Fukuzawa's thinking about civilization. Together with *An Encouragement of Learning*, which was published in separate chapters between 1872 and 1876, the work marks Fukuzawa's turn from translation to original writing. Bold and imaginative, it has none of the stumbling or awkward character often associated with first works. Fukuzawa was just forty when he wrote the book. For years, he had pondered the subject of civilization and the nature of Japan's civilization in relation to that of the West. *Outline* was at once a statement of the views he had arrived at during the process of his earlier translations and a response to books he had read more recently. It bursts with ideas he had hitherto refrained from inserting into his translations. Once the book was published, although the schema of stages and the goal of civilization remained orienting

100

principles in his thought, Fukuzawa's attention turned to other, more immediate and timely issues.[1]

In thinking about *Outline*, we must bear in mind how Fukuzawa's personal situation had changed. When he translated Burton in 1868 and Mitchell in 1869, he was adrift in a sea of uncertainty. His job at the Tokugawa foreign ministry had vanished with the collapse of the bakufu, and it was not clear what he would do next. After the Meiji Restoration in 1868, he was offered various positions in the new Meiji officialdom, but he turned them down. He bet on his ability to go it alone, though it was still unclear whether the little domain school he had founded would survive the transition to the new era, and whether he would be able to support himself by writing. By 1875, however, these uncertainties had disappeared; his finances were secure and his reputation established. During periods of need he was able to subsidize his school with the income from his writings. He wrote to a friend in 1873: "I have become quite affluent. As far as wealth is concerned, I have no reason to envy even ministers of state."[2] The new stability in his life was reflected in the ease, self-confidence, and flashes of wit in *Outline*. He enjoyed writing the book, or so it seems to the casual reader.

Japan, too, had changed. Fukuzawa, shocked by the military victories of Chōshū and Satsuma that had led to the Restoration, despaired at the prospect of government by "expel-the-barbarian" xenophobes, whom he had bitterly opposed during the pre-Restoration era. But to his surprise and immense satisfaction, the new government rid itself of the xenophobes, or those who still clung to their xenophobia, and turned to a broad program of Westernizing reforms. It upheld the treaties with a toughness never displayed by the former Tokugawa rulers. It abolished the daimyo domains, and then set about to abolish the samurai class—just those institutions that Fukuzawa had viewed as "feudal" roadblocks to progress.

In Fukuzawa's eyes, by 1875 the government had done just about all that a modernizing government could do. The reforms "from above" were almost complete. Japan, he felt, had reached a juncture where further change must depend on the transformation of the Japanese people through learning and education. This critical judgment of Japan's situation was the basis for his overall argument in *Outline:* the Japanese people must advance by absorbing Western civilization but they must

Fukuzawa Yukichi in Tokyo in 1876, a year after publishing *Outline of Theories of Civilization*.

keep Japan independent while doing so. All of the polemics in the book return to this single proposition. Within the larger argument, to be sure, Fukuzawa presented a variety of subarguments concerning the nature of civilization, traditional Japanese civilization, and the behavior of Western nations toward other areas of the world.

Finally, it should be stressed at the outset that while Fukuzawa admired the West and believed that Japan should emulate its achievements, he was not infatuated with it. His concern was always with the "civilization that had first appeared in the West," and not with "Western civilization." The distinction is a fine one and often blurs, but it is

nonetheless critical. It helps explain his indifference to Western literature, art, music, and religion—fields not intrinsic, he felt, to the attainment of civilization. The distinction also helps explain his deep appreciation of new schools, libraries, hospitals, schools for the deaf and
blind, and poorhouses. Like steam engines, such institutions were a
necessary part of civilization and would propel Japan along the path toward it.

Western Civilization as the Goal

The first three chapters of *Outline* present Fukuzawa's reflections on
Mitchell and Burton—with a few ideas from Henry Thomas Buckle
and François Guizot mixed in. In the second chapter, titled "Making
Western Civilization Our Goal," he describes the stages (he used the
term *yowai*, or ages) of civilization. The earliest stage was barbarism,
which, he wrote, could still be found in Australia and Africa.[3]

> In the first age, humans have neither fixed dwellings nor regular
> supplies of food. They group together for convenience, and when
> convenience ends, they scatter without a trace. Even if they settle
> in one place, engage in farming and fishing, and do not lack the
> basic necessities of life, they are still ignorant of the mechanical
> arts. They may have writing, but they have no body of learning.
> They fear the forces of nature, rely on the arbitrary favors and
> judgments of others, and passively wait upon accidental fortune or
> misfortune, unable to act on their own behalf. This stage is called
> barbarism (*yaban*). It is far removed from civilization.[4]

The second stage, to which Japan belonged, along with China, Turkey, and other Asian countries, was the "half-civilized."

> In the second age of civilization, agriculture is well developed and
> the basic necessities are secured. Houses are built, cities and vil-
> lages are established, and there is the outward semblance of a
> state. But if one probes deeply, one finds that shortcomings are le-
> gion. Learning flourishes, but few devote themselves to practical
> studies. In human relations, doubts, suspicions and jealousies run
> deep, yet in discussions of the principles of things, the courage to

raise doubts and correct errors is lacking. Artisans are adept at im-
itation but inept at the creation of new things; they know how to
cultivate the old, but not how to improve it. Society is not without
rules (kisoku), but overwhelmed by custom, a proper system of law
is not achieved. This age is called half-civilized (hankai), and still
falls short of civilization.[5]

The third and highest stage was "civilization." The "enlightened"
phase of civilized society was subsumed under this term.

In the third age, men cleverly frame the laws of the universe yet
act freely within them. Their temperament is open and bright, and
they do not adhere blindly to old customs. They have self-control
and do not depend on arbitrary favors by others. They spontaneously cultivate virtue and refine their knowledge. They neither
yearn for the past, nor are they complacent with the present. Not
content with small gains, they plan for great future deeds; they
go forward and do not retreat, nor do they stop when they attain
a goal. Their scholarship is not empty of substance; they have
discovered the basis of invention. Manufacturing and commerce
grow daily, deepening the fount of human happiness. Knowledge
is used today, and what is not used is carried over for future plans.
This is the present state of civilization, advanced far beyond the
barbarous and the half-civilized states.[6]

Fukuzawa presented this Mitchell-like schema without the slightest
hesitation. He stated categorically: "These designations of civilized,
half-civilized, and barbarous are used throughout the world and are accepted by all the peoples of the world. Why do they accept them? Because they are true, supported by evidence that cannot be doubted."[7]
    Later in the Outline, he compared "half-civilized" (and by that token,
"half-barbarous") Japan with the "civilized" West, and concluded that
the West was superior in nearly all respects.

If we compare the knowledge of Japanese and Westerners,
whether in learning, technology, commerce, or industry, from the
greatest to the least, in one hundred cases or in one thousand,
not even in one instance are we superior. We can neither oppose

them nor think of doing so. Aside from the most stupid people in the land, no one thinks that our learning, technology, commerce, and industry are on a par with theirs. Would anyone presume to compare our carts with their steam locomotives, or our swords with their rifles? While we recite theories about the *yin* and *yang* and the five elements, they have discovered the sixty elements. While we divine lucky and unlucky days by astrology, they plot the courses of comets and study the composition of the sun and the moon. While we think we live on an immobile and flat earth, they know that it is spherical and moves. While we regard Japan as the sacred islands of the gods, they race around the world, discovering new lands and founding new nations . . . On all these counts, in comparison to the West, there is nothing in which we can take pride. The only things we Japanese can boast of are our natural products and the scenery of our mountains and seas.[8]

It follows, Fukuzawa concluded, that "those who would plan for their country's progress toward civilization must take European civilization as their goal and use it as the standard for judging all matters." Only then will Japan be able to progress and maintain its independence. He underlined his unequivocal affirmation of the European model with the words, "Let no scholar mistake my intent!"[9]

Fukuzawa further elaborated the concept of civilization. In his third chapter, "The True Purpose of Civilization," he presented a Montesquieu-like conception of civilization as a coherent and spiritually united whole—a conception that went beyond the American geographers and Burton. He began by comparing an entire civilization to its components. Following an argument in François Guizot's *General History of Civilization in Europe,* he wrote that the sole criterion for judging any part of a civilization is the extent to which it served to advance civilization as a whole. Guizot had compared civilization to a "great drama," to "an ocean into which rivers flow," to a "grand emporium of the people" where "all the powers of its existence are stored up." When Fukuzawa came to Guizot's simile of a "great drama," he let his imagination take wing:

Civilization is like a great theater, with political institutions, literature, commerce, and so on, as the actors. Each actor performs his special skill and does his part in the production. An actor is called skilled who, in conformance with the dramatic intent of the play, displays true emotions and delights the audience. An actor is called awkward who misses his cues, fumbles his lines, whose laughter rings false, whose sobs are without feeling, and thereby causes the play to lose its significance.[10]

Each component of a civilization must be appropriate to the "dramatic intent" or "spirit" that pervades the whole and gives the civilization its distinct character.

He then expanded on the notion of spiritual coherence:

What is this spirit *(seishin)?* It is the ethos of a people *(jinmin no kifū)*. This ethos can neither be bought nor sold, nor can human efforts quickly create it. It permeates a nation's entire population and manifests itself in every aspect of national life, yet its shape cannot be seen with the eyes and it is extremely difficult even to know where it exists.

I will try, nevertheless, to say where it can be found. If scholars read widely in world history, compare present-day Asia and Europe, and put aside such factors as geography and products, ordinances and laws, levels of scholarship and technology, and religious differences, they will inevitably discover that what separates the two continents is a kind of amorphous entity *(mukei na mono)*. It is extremely difficult to describe what this entity is. If nourished, it will grow to encompass all things on this earth. If suppressed, it will wither until all traces of it disappear. Advancing or retreating, waxing or waning, it changes without cease. And yet, though it seems almost like a will-o'-the-wisp, if we look at its manifestations in Asia and Europe at present, we know with certainty that it is not illusory.

He continued:

If we wish to attach a name to this entity, we may call it the ethos of a nation's people. In regard to time, we call it the trend of the times *(jisei)*. In regard to persons, we call it the human mind *(jinshin)*. In regard to countries, we speak of it as national customs *(kokuzoku)*, or as the national opinion *(kokuron)*. The so-called spirit of civilization is nothing less than the combination of these several things. It is this spirit of civilization that makes Asia differ from Europe.[11]

It was from this larger perspective that Fukuzawa argued that Japan must strive to transform the spirit of its civilization and grasp the essential spirit of the West, and not merely build stone buildings, iron bridges, and warships—the "externals of civilization." But how was this to be done? If the spirit of a civilization is formless and not easily changed by human efforts, where and how should the Japanese start? Most of *Outline* was taken up with his answer to this question.

Sugarcoating the Pill

To prescribe the adoption of European civilization and the abandonment of substantial parts of one's own is a bitter medicine. To make the prescription more palatable, Fukuzawa prefaced both of the arguments mentioned earlier with an introductory chapter, "Establishing a Basis for Argumentation." In it, he explained to his readers that "civilization" is a relative term.

> The civilized are civilized relative to the half-civilized, but even the half-civilized must be called civilized relative to the barbarous. For instance, the condition of China at present must be called half-civilized relative to the West. But if we compare China to the countries of southern Africa, or, more immediately, if we compare the people of Japan to the Ezo [Ainu], then both China and Japan are civilized. Furthermore, though we call the Western countries civilized, it is only in the present world that they merit that rank . . . Thousands of years hence, if by chance the world's peoples greatly advance in knowledge and virtue and arrive at a utopian order *(taihei anraku no kyokudo)*, the present-day condition of Western countries will seem pitifully barbarous. From this perspective, the potentials of civilization have no bounds, and we must not be content with the Western civilization as it is today.[12]

Burton had written that civilization was by its nature continuously advancing, and that it would be much improved in the future. Guizot made the same point in his *General History of Civilization in Europe:*

"Civilization is properly a relative term. It refers to a certain state of mankind as distinguished from barbarism." "Society and civilization are still in their childhood . . . however great the distance they have advanced, that which they have before them is incomparably, is infinitely, greater." Fukuzawa took this argument a step further and suggested that the preeminence of the West was recent and may not necessarily be permanent. In the preface to *Outline* he broached the possibility that Japan, after catching up, might even move ahead. The effect of the sudden contact with the West, he wrote, made the Japanese "dissatisfied with their own civilization" and "eager to make their civilization like that of the West. They expect, eventually, either to obtain parity with the West, or to ultimately surpass it . . . Truly, it is as if the coming of the Americans during the 1850s kindled a fire in our hearts which, once ablaze, will never be extinguished."[13]

The argument for the relative nature of civilization was a start, but Fukuzawa continued to puzzle over what arguments might persuade his countrymen to Westernize. In 1876, a year after the publication of *Outline*, in response to his critics, or in anticipation of their criticism, he wrote an essay titled "Methodic Doubt and Selective Judgment."[14] One point he made was that the West had advanced its civilization by systematically doubting established truths. Galileo, Newton, and James Watt had questioned beliefs concerning the natural world. Thomas Clarkson had criticized the morality of slavery, and Luther had challenged the false teachings of Rome. In each instance, the West had arrived at a new truth by following "a zigzag course between competing interpretations." In contrast, the countries of Asia had thus far been unable to achieve intellectual progress because they lacked this ability to question accepted beliefs.[15]

A second point, which he presented with a touch of humor, was that the adoption of civilization from the West did not mean imitating every little detail of Western custom. During the early Meiji period, Fukuzawa was viewed as the outstanding proponent of "civilization and enlightenment" thought. But in this essay, he cleverly distanced himself from those he labeled the "schoolmasters of enlightenment" (*kaika sensei*)—those who "believe in the new with the same blind faith in which they believed in the old."

What if Westerners bathed daily and Japanese bathed only once or twice a month? The *kaika sensei* would say that civilized and enlightened people bathe often, cleanse their pores, and obey the laws of hygiene, and that uncivilized Japanese do not understand these principles. What if Japanese kept chamber pots in their bedrooms to store up their urine, and did not wash their hands when they left the toilet, and Westerners got up and went to the toilet, even in the middle of the night, and always washed their hands afterwards? The same critics would say that enlightened persons place a high value on cleanliness, while unenlightened persons do not know the meaning of the word.[16]

Conversely, he mused, what if the Japanese used cloth handkerchiefs and not disposable handkerchiefs made of paper, what if they dangled gold rings from their pierced ears, wore corsets that constrict the waist and damage health, or needed locks to protect their homes from robbers? What would the *kaika sensei* say then? Would they find some way of praising practices that were obviously bad? Fukuzawa was telling his readers that systematic doubt can also be directed at the foibles of the West.

At the end of the essay, Fukuzawa turned from light humor to "the loftier subject of religion." He compared Shinran, the medieval Japanese Buddhist reformer, to Luther, who had attacked the Christianity of Rome and established the Protestant sect. How would the "schoolmasters of enlightenment" have judged these two religious figures, he asked, if their nationalities had been reversed? Would they not have praised Shinran, who sought salvation for all sentient beings, endured great personal hardships, opposed killing, and won for his sect the hearts of a majority of his countrymen? And might they not have condemned Luther, who, despite the Christian precept to love thine enemy, had unleashed a century or more of wars and slaughter? In the Reformation struggles, Fukuzawa averred, the Catholic church was like a tiger and the Protestants like wolves.

Having made his point, Fukuzawa might have left well enough alone. But he probed further. Was the issue really that simple? Perhaps the two religions were composed of fundamentally different cultural elements (*genso o koto ni suru*) from the start. Did Shinran and Luther represent different levels of virtue? Or was it that religious strife played out differently in barbarous and civilized lands? Even after thinking about these matters for a long time, Fukuzawa confessed that he remained puzzled. At the time, no one else in Japan posed such questions.

Arguments for the relativity of civilizations and amusing observations about the practices of the West may have sugarcoated the pill, but the medicine Fukuzawa prescribed remained the same: abandon the outdated ideas and institutions of Japan, and with a few minor exceptions, take in those of the West. He maintained this position with only slight modifications for the rest of his life. In an 1885 editorial, for example, he argued that Japan should "withdraw from Asia" and its backward civilization, and "move in step with the civilization of Europe."[17]

The Theory and Japan

How, then, did Fukuzawa apply the theory of stages to Japan? This would seem to be an easy question, given the wealth of historical data presented in *Outline*. But the answer is not as obvious as it might first appear.

The schema of stages was designed to explain European history to Europeans. The essential question was "how we got to where we are today and how our condition compares to that of the rest of the world." The schema focused on transitions from one kind of society to another: from the barbarism of post-Roman feudal society to the half-civilized state of high feudalism and feudal monarchy, and then on to the higher civilization that was ushered in by the scientific revolution of the seventeenth century, the Enlightenment of the eighteenth, and the industrial revolution of the nineteenth. European history was eventful and the pace of change rapid.

The schema of stages, however, was far less useful in explaining Japan's past. As Fukuzawa noted in his reply to Erasmus Peshine Smith, there was no evidence (in 1875) that Japan had ever been a hunting and gathering society, or that it had ever been pastoral. Nor is it clear from Fukuzawa's writing when the "half-civilized" stage began. He never treats the question systematically. He states that the Japanese of ancient times *(inishie)* were barbarous and illiterate *(yaban fubun)*. But he also writes that ancient Japan, as depicted in the earliest histories, was already agricultural—a technology often associated with the "half-civilized" state. Writing of religion, Fukuzawa comments that the coming of Buddhist and Confucian teachings "rescued our people from barbarism and brought them to today's level of civilization." From these scattered references, it would appear that Japan entered the "half-

civilized" state during the seventh or eighth centuries, when it established relations with China. And it was still only "half-civilized,"
Fukuzawa asserted, in the mid-nineteenth century. But if all of Japanese history from the Nara period to the Tokugawa represents a single
stage, then a theory that deals with transitions from one stage to another has little explanatory power.

None of this mattered to Fukuzawa. He was not primarily concerned
to explain Japan's past. He saw the schema, rather, as a universal history. It permitted comparisons between Japan and other countries of
the world, as earlier Japanese histories had not. His purpose was to illuminate Japan's future. He did this by contrasting Japan's present, and
that part of the past that still lived on in the present, with Japan's future,
as represented by the civilization of Europe. For Fukuzawa, the schema
was like a crystal ball.

Let us consider several examples. One target of his polemic was the
samurai spirit, which in 1875 was still idealized by many in Japan.
Fukuzawa saw this spirit as a part of Japan's old feudal mentality that
was inadequate to the needs of the modern age. It was a part of the past
that, in some measure, still lived on in the present. To make the point,
in *An Encouragement of Learning* he contrasted the behavior of Japanese
samurai of the mid-sixteenth century with French soldiers during the
Franco-Prussian War of 1871. Imagawa Yoshimoto was a great feudal
lord and a famous general. In 1560, his troops were ranged against the
armies of Oda Nobunaga. But when Imagawa was captured and be-
headed, his troops, without doing battle, "scattered like little spiders,"
and his once powerful domain "collapsed in a day and vanished without
a trace." In contrast, even after Louis Napoleon was captured at the
onset of the war with Prussia, French troops fought on valiantly until a
treaty was signed, and France "survived as of old." The critical difference was between a feudal army personally loyal to a leader but not to a
country, and a citizen army whose members took upon themselves
the responsibility for their nation. The "civilized" French possessed a
"spirit of independence" *(dokuritsu no kiryoku)* that the retainers of
Imagawa had lacked, and that Fukuzawa felt the Japanese still lacked in
1875.[18]

A famous incident in 1701 in which forty-seven loyal retainers
avenged their daimyo lord was Fukuzawa's second example of the weakness of the samurai spirit. He must have enjoyed taking this most fa-

mous example of samurai loyalty and turning it on its head in *An Encouragement of Learning*. The details of the tale were well known to all
Japanese and had long furnished materials for Kabuki drama, puppet
theater, and popular stories. In his analysis, however, Fukuzawa ignored the thrilling saga of heroic action and looked at the numbers.
Why, he asked, in an age when loyalty was in full bloom, did only forty-
seven persons in a domain of seventy thousand remain loyal to the end?
Applying that ratio to Japan's population of thirty million in 1875, and
discounting by 30 percent to account for the erosion of the loyalty
ethic since the 1700s, Fukuzawa reasoned that in the Japan of his day,
only 14,100 persons would step forward to defend Japan in battle.
"Will such a number suffice to defend Japan? Even a child of three can
do the calculation!" In the contemporary world, the ethic of moral sub-
servience to feudal lords, he concluded, can never substitute for the
spirit of educated and independent citizens who identify their own welfare with the fortunes of their nation.

> To protect our country from foreign nations, we must establish a
> spirit of freedom and independence throughout the entire coun-
> try. With no distinction between noble and base, high and low,
> learned and ignorant, blind and sighted, each person must take it
> upon himself to fulfill his duty as a citizen. Englishmen love En-
> gland as their native land; Japanese love Japan as theirs. Since the
> land is ours and not another's, we love it as we do our homes. For
> the sake of our country, we must willingly sacrifice not only prop-
> erty but our very lives. This is the great principle of repaying the
> country.[19]

Another target of Fukuzawa's polemic was the Japanese emperor.
Overall, Fukuzawa's judgment was that the emperor, as traditionally
conceived within Japan's "half-civilized" society, was incompatible with
the requirements of a rational "civilization." But he recognized that the
subject was complex and approached it from three different angles.
The first pointed out that the Japanese emperor institution was not all
bad. The second argued that the emperor be made over into a modern
monarch. The third, which will be treated somewhat later, suggested
that the emperor was not really that important.
The first argument posed the question of why the Japanese had been

able to rid themselves of their ancient regime and set out on the road to civilization, whereas the Chinese had not. His answer implicitly made the point that significant differences could exist between nations at the same "stage" of history. It also suggested that the Japanese emperor's role in contemporary government should be limited. Both China and Japan, Fukuzawa wrote, had begun with systems of absolute rule, that is, with theocracies in which the title to rule was bestowed by heaven. In China, the system had remained unchanged into recent times: the emperor had remained both the most powerful figure and the most sacred. But in Japan, from Kamakura times, power and sacredness had come apart. The shogun had the power while the emperor had the sacredness. The separation of the roles of shogun and emperor turned out to be an "accidental stroke of good fortune," since the tension between them "allowed room for the rise of dissident thought and the play of reason." It provided the leeway by which a coalition of domains could use the emperor against the Tokugawa shogun and carry out the Meiji Restoration. Without that tension, "there would be no Japan as it exists today." The same play of reason, he continued, enables Japan to adopt Western civilization more easily than China. But, he warned, this good fortune might be lost if "imperial scholars" have their way and the emperor is permitted to wield both political and religious power.[20]

Fukuzawa's second argument was a flank attack on the traditional mythological conception of the emperor. Such a conception, he argued, was simply incompatible with the rationality of a modern "civilization." His particular animus in these arguments was directed against kōgaku or "Emperor Studies," a school of thought whose ideas derived from the "National Studies" (kokugaku) teachings of Hirata Atsutane (1776–1843). He also opposed the Shinto-tinged Confucian ideology of the old Mito domain. The two schools differed in most respects— Hirata was dead against Confucian teachings. But they agreed that the Japanese emperor was descended from the sun goddess Amaterasu, and that this divine bloodline legitimized imperial rule and constituted the basis for the political duties of the Japanese as subjects. The relationship between the Japanese people, the emperor, and the Shinto gods was sometimes referred to as the Japanese "national polity" or kokutai. Fukuzawa's goal was to strip the emperor of his Shinto trappings and make him into a modern monarch.

In his analysis, Fukuzawa completely ignored the premise of divine descent. It was as if he were quietly informing his readers that such old-fashioned mumbo jumbo was unworthy of their consideration. Instead, he described the emperor institution in terms of three separate and secular elements: national polity, legitimacy, and bloodline.

"National polity," he argued, means national independence and the ties that bind together the people of an independent nation. Having such a polity, he maintained, is not unique to Japan. By definition, every independent nation has one. But any nation that loses its independence also loses its national polity. India lost its *kokutai* when it became a colony of Britain; the American Indians lost theirs when white settlers drove them from their lands. "Legitimacy" is necessary for any government to rule. Whether it was originally established by force or by peaceful means does not matter as long as the people accept the government as legitimate. The rationale for legitimacy may be feudal, monarchical, parliamentary, or religious, and will vary over time. As long as a country does not become subject to an external power, changes in the rationale for rule have no effect on the national polity. As an example, Fukuzawa noted that in English history, from the time of William III to the present, the nation preserved its independence despite sweeping changes in rationale that occurred so gradually as to be almost imperceptible. "Bloodline," the third element, is separate from the other two and mainly a matter of biology. The form of succession within monarchies may be from father to son, from brother to brother, or may involve some other relative. Succession disputes, Fukuzawa noted, are common throughout the world.

Applying these definitions to Japan, Fukuzawa observed that its imperial bloodline was old and unbroken; this, he allowed, is "something special," but not terribly important. The legitimacy of Japanese governments has changed any number of times, and will doubtless change again in the future. This is what happens to governments and, in a larger sense, it does not matter either. What counts is that Japan has never been conquered; it has never lost its national polity to a foreign power. To preserve this independence, he concluded, Japan must strengthen itself by quickly adopting the "civilization" that had been attained in the West.[21]

Fukuzawa made his argument more concrete by distinguishing between the false and the true rationales providing legitimacy for governments. Claims to a false authority *(kyoi)* were common in barbarous

times. They were appropriate to superstitious peoples who were ignorant of nature and in awe of its external forms. A ruler might claim that
heaven had given him a mandate to rule; another might say that his an-
cestor had climbed a holy mountain and spoken directly to God. Based
on such irrational claims, rulers established theocracies. In China, "the
son of heaven" ruled with a combination of punishments and "rites and
music." The Chinese people had no recourse but to pray that he would
be benevolent. But whether the exercise of such a false authority was
benevolent or tyrannical, theocratic rule left no room for the play of intelligence.[22]

But superstition has declined in the civilized world of today.

> The only means to govern the people at present is to create com-
> pacts based on reason and protect them with a government of true
> authority *(jitsui)*. In the present age everyone knows that building
> an altar and praying for rain will not bring rain to end a seven-year
> drought. Even if the ruler himself prays for a bountiful harvest,
> the laws of chemistry will not change. That the prayers of man-
> kind will not increase the harvest by a single grain is something
> that even school children understand.[23]

Fukuzawa cited England as an example that Japan might profitably
follow. On entering a more rational age, England successfully made the
transition from an old-style, despotic monarchy to a government em-
phasizing the rights of the people. This shift not only guaranteed the
survival of its royal house, but also strengthened its national polity, that
is, its national independence.[24]

It is a commentary on the openness of the early Meiji era that Fukuzawa could deconstruct the Shinto persona of the emperor and blithely
ignore the mythological arguments of his ideological foes. Most of his
readers, one imagines, understood what he was doing and did not dis-
approve. Despite the "imperial" Restoration of 1868, an unassailable
"emperor ideology" had not yet formed. By the 1880s, however, when
Fukuzawa wrote the essays "On The Imperial House" *(Teishitsuron)*
and "On Honoring the Emperor" *(Sonnōron)*, the climate of opinion
had changed. His analysis was essentially the same as in 1875, but his
presentation was more circumspect. Indeed, it takes a careful reading
to grasp his true views.[25] After the 1890 *Imperial Rescript on Education*,

which proclaimed the imperial throne to "be coeval with heaven and earth," public deconstructions of Japan's divine emperor became strictly taboo.

Buckle's Theory of Civilization

Fukuzawa presented a second theory of civilization in the four middle chapters of *Outline*. The theory came from Henry Thomas Buckle's *History of Civilization in England*. Unlike his use of Mitchell and Burton in the earlier chapters, Fukuzawa was more selective, accepting some ideas and rejecting others. He also added ideas of his own and drew examples from the histories of Japan and China.[26]

Henry Thomas Buckle (1821–1862) was the son of a rich London merchant. A sickly youth, he received little formal schooling and never attended college or university, but he was unquestionably brilliant with a scholarly turn of mind. Before the age of twenty, he attained renown as a chess master. During his lifetime, he was reputed to have mastered nineteen languages. But from his youth, his greatest interest was history, and it became his lifework. Determined to do for history what natural scientists had done for physics, he set out to write a history of civilization in terms of the universal laws of nature and the human mind. The first volume of his planned sixteen-volume work was published to great acclaim in 1857, the second in 1861. He died a year later at age forty-one in Damascus, where he was traveling for his health.

Buckle's theory of history began with the proposition that all history "must be the fruit of a double action; an action of external phenomena on the mind, and another action of the mind on the phenomena . . . Thus we have man modifying nature, and nature modifying man." Of these processes, Buckle argued that for most of human history nature had prevailed. Nature's active forces, he specified, are "soil, food, climate, and the general aspects of nature." By "general aspects of nature," he meant those aspects that excite "the imagination" and give rise to "those innumerable superstitions which are the greatest obstacle to advancing knowledge." Outside of Europe, such superstitions have proved to be "insuperable." "No nation has yet overcome them." This was because "in all civilizations exterior to Europe, all nature conspired to increase the authority of the imaginative faculties and weaken the authority of the reasoning ones."[27] In his view, the religions of India exemplified the triumph of the imagination. For Buckle, the goddess Kali was the product of a "tropical imagination":

> She has a body of dark blue . . . [and] four arms, with one of which she carries the skull of a giant; her tongue protrudes, and hangs lollingly from her mouth; round her waist are the hands of her victims; and her neck is adorned with human heads strung together in a ghastly row.[28]

Europe, however, was different. It was smaller and colder than tropical lands, and had "a less exuberant soil." Consequently, in Europe, "the tendency of natural phenomena is, on the whole, to limit the imagination, and embolden the understanding." This gave rise to that "bold, inquisitive, scientific spirit which is constantly advancing and on which all future progress must depend." The civilization of Europe, Buckle wrote, "has diverged from all others that preceded it."[29]

Fukuzawa accepted as a fact the notion that Europe had diverged from others and raced ahead. Even before reading Buckle, he had reached the conclusion that Europe, for the moment, represented civilization. But he rejected Buckle's climate-based argument. Japan, like Europe, was in the temperate zone. Appeals to a "tropical imagination" did not explain why Japan had not developed the same bold scientific spirit as Europe.

A second part of Buckle's theory was that entire societies, not individuals, must be studied to understand the mental laws that shape history. Human actions, he held, are the result of social antecedents—not of a capricious free will or of supernatural interventions. To study the "mental laws" and regularities that proceed from these antecedents, he recommended the use of statistical data gathered by impartial bodies. Murder and suicide are intensely personal acts, yet such acts, year after year, occur in stable and predictable numbers. Marriages would seem to depend on the personal feelings of young men and women; yet invariably, when the price of corn rises, their frequency declines, and when the price drops, their frequency rises.

Fukuzawa liked this second argument better. So in *Outline* he cited Buckle and his *History of Civilization in England* by name and presented Buckle's findings on murder, suicide, and marriage. (The only change he made was to substitute the price of rice for that of corn.) The mar-

kets of Tokyo, Fukuzawa added, exhibited similar regularities. The
vender of rice cakes has no knowledge of who will buy and who will
not; the outcome would seem to depend on individual whims. But by
evening, his stock is usually gone. To understand the fixed laws *(teisoku)*
that lead to this result, "the minds of the entire body of townspeople"
must be studied. Ultimate causes are not always obvious.[30] If the entire
body of townsmen is critical—not just the few individuals who happened to buy rice cakes—then for larger historical events, it is the spirit
or the level of civilization of an entire nation that is critical (not just the
ability of a handful of leaders).

Fukuzawa extended Buckle's logic to demonstrate that great men do
not shape the history of nations. As was often the case, he began his argument with an analogy. A nation's leader, he wrote, is like the captain
of a steamship, and the people are like the engine; even the most skilled
captain cannot make a ship go faster than the power of its engines. In
the American Revolutionary War, the colonists won because of their
spirit of independence; their victory did not depend on George Washington and a handful of other leaders. Had Washington lost the war,
the independent spirit would have given rise to other Washingtons
and eventually independence would have been gained. Similarly, in the
Franco-Prussian War, the outcome was determined by the strength of
the Prussian spirit and the weakness of the French, and not by any difference between Bismarck and Napoleon III. Carried away by this
logic, Fukuzawa gave an even more extreme example:

> Let me state this more clearly. Suppose that Washington became
> the emperor of China and Wellington was appointed as the sho-
> gun to lead the Chinese army in battle against the British troops.
> Which side would lose and which would gain victory? Even if the
> Chinese warships and cannons were mighty, they would be de-
> feated by the matchlocks and schooners of the British soldiers.
> Victory in war depends not on generals or weaponry but on the
> spirit of the people *(jinmin ippan no kiryoku)*.[31]

Fukuzawa's use of Buckle's argument was not unrelated to his view of
Japan's needs in 1875. Before 1871, Fukuzawa's exhortations had been
aimed primarily at Japan's leaders. He chafed at the government's un-
willingness to act decisively. But after the abolition of the domains in

1871, and even more so after the reforms that began in 1872 and 1873 (conscription, land tax reform, and the pensioning off of samurai), he felt that the government had done just about all that a government could do. He recognized that the government had men of ability, but what Japan needed was a modern citizenry, a people who would respond to reform in an enlightened fashion. Further progress depended on educating the people and raising the level of their civilization. Further progress depended on the spirit of the entire nation, and not on a few leaders.

Buckle's third argument, which for Fukuzawa was his most important, analyzed "civilization" and the "mental laws of progress" in terms of their moral and intellectual components. The moral component, Buckle stated, has a "more immediate relation to our duties," and the intellectual, "to our knowledge." For civilization to progress, both are essential.

> To be willing to perform our duty is the moral part; to know how to perform it is the intellectual part; the closer the two parts are knit together . . . the more completely will the scheme of our life be accomplished, and the more securely shall we lay a foundation for the further advancement of mankind.[32]

Fukuzawa accepted this proposition wholeheartedly. In fact, he used the term *chitoku* (intelligence and virtue) in the chapter title of each of the four middle chapters of *Outline*. He wrote:

> To determine the nature of a civilization, we must first perceive the spirit that informs it. That spirit is a manifestation of the intelligence [or knowledge] and virtue *(chitoku)* of its people. It advances or retreats, grows or diminishes, without cease, and constitutes the source of all change in that nation. Once this spirit is understood, all matters in that country will become clear—as easy to weigh as finding an object in one's pocket.[33]

But Buckle then went on to distinguish between the two. Moral truths are "stationary." There is "nothing to be found in the world which has undergone so little change as those great dogmas of which moral systems are composed." Intellectual truths, in contrast, are constantly advancing, and are "quite sufficient to account for the extraordinary progress that, during several centuries, Europe has continued to make." The rise of the sciences and invention in Europe enabled humans to take control of nature for the first time in world history.[34]

Fukuzawa embraced this argument because it magnified the importance of knowledge as the quicksilver dimension of progress. Buckle, in effect, provided a theoretical justification for the emphasis on learning that Fukuzawa had already arrived at during the 1860s and had stressed in the early chapters of *An Encouragement of Learning*. Though this was not his intention, by singling out this factor Buckle had suggested a how-to-do-it or where-to-start instruction to developing nations that was absent from Mitchell or Burton.

It is beyond the scope of this book to detail Fukuzawa's many and varied applications of the distinction between virtue and intelligence. He plays and replays similar themes like contrapuntal voices in a fugue. Two of his discussions, however, are particularly pertinent to the issue of civilization. The first treats the Meiji Restoration as an eruption of rationality and downplays the significance of the emperor. The second reviews the sweep of human history and restates Fukuzawa's earlier view of the relationship between rationality and government.

The overall argument in *Outline* is that Japan is backward and must change. The country's "half-civilized" society is ill-equipped to deal with the challenges presented by the "civilized" West. But if Japan was actually so backward, how had Tokugawa rule been overthrown in 1868 and why had the Meiji reforms begun? Fukuzawa began his explanation by reaffirming the dearth of rationality during the early centuries of Tokugawa rule:

> For long years, the people of our country suffered under the yoke of despotism *(sensei no bōsei)*. Hereditary rulers *(monbatsu)* were the source of authority. They determined whether men of talent were used or not used. Oppressed by these conditions, within the entire country the forces of intelligence could not move.[35]

By the early nineteenth century, however, doctors, writers, samurai, Buddhist and Shinto priests, and others with education had become discontented. They could not criticize the system directly, but they could complain obliquely of injustices and ills. How long it would have taken these early glimmerings of intelligence to win out in the absence of a foreign intrusion is unclear, but just as intelligence was gaining a precarious foothold, Perry came to Japan. Fukuzawa described the shock of his arrival in the passage cited at the beginning of this chapter. Knowledge of the existence and strength of the Western powers gave a jolt to the intellectual powers of the people. It acted as a catalyst that enabled the "intelligent minority" to overcome the "ignorant major-ity," and it was this minority's dissatisfactions and new knowledge of the world that fueled the movement "to overthrow the bakufu." The political change of 1868 was labeled a "restoration," but in reality, it had nothing to do with the emperor.

The return to the old imperial system (ōsei fukko) was not accom-plished by the influence of the imperial house; the imperial house merely lent its name to the forces of intelligence within the coun-try. The abolition of the domains and the establishment of a cen-tralized government (haihan chiken) was not a decisive act taken by the government leaders; the government leaders were merely serving the forces of intelligence within the country.[36]

Had the restoration, in fact, been about returning the government to the emperor, it would have ended in 1868. But the forces of intelli-gence carried it forward in line with their own interests. Fukuzawa put this in numerical terms: of the five million in the samurai class, only a tenth were active in the restoration. Excluding women and children, the number is even smaller. Despite this, the forces of intelligence were able to prevail because the conservative majority lacked talent. This is not rare in history, he suggested: "To generalize, those who favor the turmoil of reform have intelligence but lack money. Whether one looks at past or present history, it is always this way."[37]

Fukuzawa's second argument reviewed all human civilization in terms of human intelligence. In one sense, he described a worldwide frame-work of evolving rationality of which the Meiji Restoration was but a single instance. The argument is notable for its offhand dismissal of Shinto beliefs that were still alive in nineteenth-century Japan.

"At the dawn of civilization (kaibyaku no hajime), when humans had just emerged from barbarism, their intelligence, like that of a child, was undeveloped." Rational thinking was absent. The people were ignorant of nature and in awe of its forces. They ascribed both fortune and mis-fortune to "supra-human causes."

Such causes gave rise to their feeling that demons and gods exist. They named the causes of calamities "evil gods" *(aku no kami)* and of nature's blessings, "good gods" *(zen no kami)*. In Japan, the myriad gods of Shinto *(yaoyorozu no kami)* were just such beings. They asked the good gods for blessings and the evil gods to spare them from calamities. Whether their entreaties would be answered or not was up to the demons and gods and not a matter of their efforts. Calling on divine powers *(shinryoku)* for help was called prayer—the so-called *kitō* of that age.[38]

And just as they feared calamities, the people feared strong rulers. Their helpless acceptance of reality as they experienced it provided support for theocracies and irrational systems of rule.

But, Fukuzawa wrote, "as learning *(jinbun)* advanced and intelligence progressed, men began to entertain doubts." Instead of relying on gods, they came to rely on their own efforts to obtain security, and they gradually lost their fear of natural disasters *(tensai)*. As a result, "about half lost the belief in the demons and gods that they had relied on only yesterday. For each step that knowledge *(chie)* advances, a measure of courage is born, a process that has no limits." Fukuzawa used Western civilization, with its steam engines, telegraph, and chemistry, to illustrate the advance of an intelligence that "gradually breaks through the boundaries of nature to discover the secrets of creation *(zōka no himitsu)*." With nature's energies harnessed to the service of man, "it need no longer be feared and worshipped." In the state of civilization, "who would worship a mountain or pray to a river!"

Fukuzawa then extended these arguments to politics. The human management of nature and the resultant spirit of self-reliance and independence led to the rejection of earlier systems of rule. Governments that are civilized, he argued, would tend to their proper functions—protecting the people, helping the weak, and restraining violence—and would not meddle unduly in the private affairs of their citizens.[39]

Guizot's Theory of Civilization

In chapters 8 and 9 of *Outline*, Fukuzawa presented a third theory of civilization, which in some respects differed from those of Burton or Buckle. In chapter 8, the "History of Western Civilization," he summarized François Guizot's *General History of Civilization in Europe*. And in chapter 9, the "History of Japanese Civilization," he used Europe as a counterpoint for an analysis of Japan.

François Guizot (1787–1874) was an influential figure in early nineteenth-century France. If Buckle was an autodidact, Guizot was a professional academician. At the age of twenty-five, he was appointed professor of modern history at the University of Paris. Following a French tradition in which scholars often played roles in public life, Guizot became the most important statesman in France during the July Monarchy (1830–1848). He was in turn education minister, ambassador to England, foreign minister, and then prime minister in 1847–1848. Among his many writings, the most famous perhaps were his multivolume histories of the English Revolution and French civilization. Both were based on a wide range of primary sources. His *General History of Civilization in Europe* was a translation of *Histoire de la Civilization en Europe*, which was based on a series of lectures he gave at his university in 1829.[40]

The book covered the major developments in European history during the fifteen centuries since the fall of Rome, and pinpointed the contribution of each development to the whole of European history. Guizot saw these centuries as "modern Europe." Among the major developments or "elements" that he listed were the personal independence of the German barbarians, the spiritual authority of the Christian church that was separate from the state, and a second type of independence introduced by feudalism. Other elements contributing variously to the cohesion and self-awareness of Europe were the Crusades, the rise of merchants in free cities, monarchy, the Protestant Reformation, the emergence of nation-states, the English and French revolutions, and the philosophical revolution of the eighteenth century. Guizot's chapters are detailed and his arguments subtle. It is not surprising that his book was widely read and translated into many languages.

But before presenting these substantive historical chapters, Guizot sketched out a theoretical framework in which he contrasted the liberty of modern Europe with the tyranny of other civilizations in the world. All other civilizations possessed a "unity of character" that "emanated from a single fact, from a single idea." "In Egypt, for example, it was the theocratic principle that took possession of society . . . In India the same phenomenon occurs . . . The monuments of Hindoo literature . . . are all struck from the same die." In such civilizations "the exclusive domination of a single principle, or at least the excessive preponderance of a single principle . . . led to tyranny."[41]

"How different to all of this is . . . the civilization of modern Europe!" In Europe, Guizot contended, the same elements existed, and the same struggle occurred between them, but no element had "sufficient force to master the others, and take sole possession of society." The "inability of any one to exclude the rest" gave rise to mutual toleration, and eventually "to that liberty which we prize so dearly."[42]

> It is this which gives to European civilization its real, its immense superiority—it is this which forms its essential, its distinctive character.
>
> European civilization has, if I may be allowed the expression, at last penetrated into the ways of eternal truth—into the scheme of Providence—it moves in the ways that God has prescribed. This is the rational principle of its superiority.[43]

Viewed from the present day, Guizot's theory seems both self-serving and a bit naive. He knew little of the world beyond Europe. All societies have checks and balances of one sort or another; the sweeping generalization that all non-European societies were peculiarly unbalanced seems untenable. Furthermore, even if the idea of a "balance" has any applicability to Europe, the question remains: why did Europe alone attain it? Guizot gave no answer. He simply asserted that it was so and that the proof lay in the facts of history. The modern idea of liberty may have first appeared in Europe, but it is hard to give all the credit to a balance of elements. Various alternative explanations seem more persuasive.

In his short chapter on the "History of Western Civilization" (*Seiyō bunmei no yurai*), Fukuzawa made no attempt to match the richness and range of Guizot's historical narrative. Fukuzawa had earlier translated histories of several European nations in the first and third volumes of *Conditions in the West* and had in mind a fairly detailed picture of Europe. So instead, he wrote what might be called a distillation of Guizot's book. He first explained the principle of "balance," and then described the contributions of each element (*genso*) or development listed by Guizot. The chapter, of not much interest to us today, was intended simply as a foil to his longer companion chapter, the "History of Japanese Civilization" *(Nihon bunmei no yurai)*.

For the chapter on Japanese history, Fukuzawa took the most dubious assumption in Guizot's theory—the idea that all civilizations other than that of Europe were unbalanced—and examined Japan from that perspective. This should not have produced a positive result, but Fukuzawa somehow made it work. In fact, the chapter is brilliant and insightful, one of the best in *Outline*.

Fukuzawa first notes that Japan's problem was not a lack of diversity. Since ancient times, Japan, like Europe, had had a variety of elements—the emperor, nobility, commoners, and religions, each of which represented principles *(setsu)* that were quite distinct. "Yet these principles were unable to stand side by side, unable to draw together and form a harmonious whole . . . Inevitably, one would always outweigh and overpower the others, preventing the others from demonstrating their true character."[44] In particular, the element that became dominant in Japan was *kenryoku*, a word that can mean "power" but also means "authority." The term he used to describe the Japanese condition was "imbalance of power" *(kenryoku no henchō)*. This imbalance, which he called a "curse," was not found solely in government, but "pervaded the entire society from the greatest to the smallest and in both public and private relationships."[45]

> If one were to describe this tendency, it is as if thousands and hundreds of scales were hung throughout Japan, and without regard to size, each scale was tilted to one side as if it had lost its balance. Or it is as if a crystal with three corners and four facets were shattered into thousands of pieces, into tens of thousands of pieces, and then reduced to powder, but the tiniest bit of powder kept its three corners and four facets. And if the powder were recombined into small pieces and then into a solid mass, it is as if it would still retain the shape of three corners and four faces.[46]

Within the family, the imbalance of power existed between husband and wife, parents and children, older and younger siblings. In the larger society, it characterized the relationship between teacher and student, lord and retainer, rich and poor, noble and baseborn, main

family and branch family. On a still larger scale, it defined the relationship between large and small domains, main temples and branch temples, main shrines and branch shrines.

After establishing political power as the dominant element in Japanese civilization, Fukuzawa went through Japanese history analyzing
developments that resembled those Guizot had identified in Europe. In
each instance, he asked whether the development represented a historical break in a European direction, and whether it disturbed the preex-
isting imbalance of authority and power. He found no such instance.
The German barbarians who invaded the late Roman empire had left
behind a legacy of freedom and autonomy *(jiyū jishu)*, but the Japanese warrior class had produced no spirit of independence and autonomy *(dokuritsu jishu)*: those above were overbearing and those below
were subservient, thereby maintaining the imbalance of power. Furthermore, the Japanese government was always in the hands of a powerful elite—Fukuzawa found little to distinguish the nobles of the Nara
and Heian periods from the warlords of the centuries that followed.
Even when a commoner rose to power, he was quite happy to leave his
own social class behind and join the elite. Internal struggles between
members of the elite were frequent, but "once someone succeeded in
gaining supreme power for his family . . . everything was settled." Consequently, "throughout the more than twenty-five centuries of Japanese history, the government has repeated the same old pattern; it was
like reading the same book, or presenting the same play, over and over
again."[47]

The condition of the common people was also unchanged by larger
events in the society. They produced; the rulers consumed. Whoever
was in charge wanted the same things—"an abundance of the five grains
and a submissive population." It made no difference to the people who
their rulers were, for their lives of drudgery remained the same. "In our
country, wars were fought between warriors and warriors, not between
peoples; they were fought between military houses, not between provinces. When the warriors of two houses opened hostilities, the people
observed from the side. They feared only the stronger force, whether it
was the enemy or their own side." To document these points, Fukuzawa gave examples similar to those in *An Encouragement of Learning.*[48]

Nor did Japanese merchants emerge as a political class, despite their
expanding role in the economy. Rather than seeking autonomy like the
"independent townsmen" of European free cities, or participating in

assemblies like the European middle class of more recent centuries, Japanese merchants either sought the protection of the ruling elite or sought to join it. They were as different from "the independent peoples of the West *(seiyō dokuritsu no jinmin)* as clay is from clouds." "From the dawn of Japanese history until the present day and throughout all of Japan, no one ever imagined the possibility of an independent citizenry *(dokuritsu shimin)*, not even in the half-formed images of a dream."[49]

Japanese religions, in contrast to Christianity, laid no claim to an independent authority. Shinto was unimportant, "never a true religious force." Buddhism may have rescued Japan from barbarism and it became an important component of Japan's civilization, but it was always an appendage of the ruling class and relied on its patronage. Even learned monks were often the protégés of emperors or shogun and were given court ranks. Their position may have been religious, but their authority was borrowed from the government.[50] Confucian teachings had also helped to civilize ancient Japan, and as they spread during the Tokugawa era, they "played a considerable role in combating the specious arguments of Buddhism and Shinto and dispelling popular superstitions."[51] Yet Confucianism was also inappropriate to the needs of Japan.

Teaching Confucianism to Japanese in ancient times was like sending a farmer's daughter to do service in a noble family. She would learn refined bearing and good manners and develop her abilities and knowledge; but she would also lose her sprightliness and become completely useless at managing a household.[52]

Furthermore, Confucian scholars, like Buddhist monks, were uniformly subservient to government. "The scholars reputed to be the most talented and capable were those who were the most skilled at upholding despotism and who best served as tools of the government." Most schools were run by the bakufu or daimyo domains, and most scholars were retainers of military lords. Even the few schools that were private served the government by teaching their students how to rule over others:

Scholars in Japan were cooped up in a cage called government. They took the cage as their universe and suffered anguish within this little universe. Fortunately, in society at large, the Chinese-type Confucian education was not widespread and the number of scholars was small. And even supposing, as their teachers wished, an unlimited number of scholars had been produced, they, too, would have been crowded together in their small cage, with no hope for employment, their resentments growing ever greater, and their suffering ever more extreme. Would that not have been pitiful beyond belief![53]

If we examine Fukuzawa's arguments (which I have oversimplified), it is not difficult to point out shortcomings. Over the years, government in Japan had changed immensely. The Tokugawa bakufu, of which the Meiji government was the heir, was far more competent than were governments during the Heian era. The Japanese people had changed as well. During the Tokugawa era, substantial numbers of Japanese became literate, with consequences that became abundantly evident in Meiji political and economic life. Merchants may not have become a political class, but over the centuries they created the market economy that was critical for economic development after 1868. Confucianism and Dutch Learning contributed to the rationality that marked Japan's response to the West after 1853. Fukuzawa himself is a shining example of profound changes within the old society.

If these objections are valid, and many more can be easily adduced, why do we find Fukuzawa's chapter of Japanese history so persuasive? Partly it is the prose: the images of thousands of scales out of kilter and of scholars cooped up in cages are fresh and compelling. But it is more a matter of realism. Even after acknowledging the ways in which Japan advanced during its history, it was still backward (Fukuzawa uses the word "*okuretaru*" or late in development) in important respects when compared with the West. That was what Fukuzawa cared about; he was single-minded in wanting Japan to catch up. He used Guizot, as he had used Buckle and the schema of stages, to dramatize the gap between Japan and the West. To do this with maximum effect, he wrote as if the imbalance were unchanging. He concluded that Japanese scholars must adopt Western civilization, break out of their cages, and become independent of government. It was their task, their mission, to create the balance that had eluded Japan in the past.

In his original writings, Fukuzawa usually addressed contemporary issues. He said as much in his autobiography, when he spoke of himself as a "diagnostician" of the Japanese body politic. In 1875, the ailment of his patient was backwardness, and the medicine he prescribed was Western learning. All of his arguments were designed to persuade the patient to take the medicine. If the patient refused the medicine, he might die—that is to say, Japan might lose its national independence.[54] During the decades after finishing *Outline*, Fukuzawa would write many more prescriptions, each addressing a different ailment.

One prescription is of particular interest in that it starkly contrasts with his interpretation of Guizot. In 1892 Fukuzawa wrote an essay titled "The Future of Our National Assembly" *(Kokkai no zento)*. Seventeen years had passed since he wrote *Outline* and just two years earlier, the Diet, which Fukuzawa saw as a milestone in Japan's advance toward civilization, had opened. The malady he diagnosed was the reluctance of the Japanese people to embrace so "foreign" an institution as representative government. The cure he prescribed was for the Japanese people to realize that the habits of local self-rule, which Fukuzawa saw as a necessary foundation for representative government, were in fact an integral part of the Japanese tradition and not at all foreign.

He began by stating that "the importation of Western civilization" after the Meiji Restoration was all to the good, but that it was "lamentable" that the West had become the standard by which the Tokugawa era was judged. "All of the evils of human society are seen as having their roots in the period of old bakufu rule; its scattered ills are noted, but the beauty of the system as a whole is ignored." The founder of the Tokugawa state, Tokugawa Ieyasu, was "not solely a man of Japan but a world hero without parallel, whether in the past or at present." The state he founded enjoyed two and a half centuries of peace thanks to his legacy, and, from "the people's learning and military matters to the one hundred practical arts, there was not one thing that did not advance."[55]

The key feature of Tokugawa society, in Fukuzawa's view, was a comprehensive system of checks and balances. The emperor offset the shogun; the daimyo counterbalanced the shogun; the samurai vassals, their lords; the merchants, the samurai; and, within the government itself, there was a balance between state councils and the inspectorate. Most important of all was the balance between the formal despotism *(rikkun sensei)* of the system and the reality of local self-rule *(jichi)*. Harsh laws were rarely applied, and the "people, unafraid of the laws, lived out their lives freely and without anxiety." "To seek a parallel, Tokugawa law was like a loan for which a promissory note had been obtained but with no pressure for repayment."[56]

> Old precedents and customs were respected, and the people were accustomed to self-rule with little interference from the government. Some local officials were appointed but many were elected. Village officials handled all aspects of relations between the people and the government. The idea of self-rule, thus, became deeply ingrained in the hearts of the people.[57]

Fukuzawa characterized this system as having an even "balance of power" *(kenryoku heikin)*. This term is the exact opposite of "imbalance of power" *(kenryoku henchō)*, the phrase he had used seventeen years earlier to characterize the same society. Earlier he had argued that the imbalance was not solely within the government but extended to the entire society; now he argued that the balance was not only in the government but had also spread to the "smallest affairs of the people" *(minkan no saiji made)*. The 180-degree turn did not mean that Fukuzawa, late in life, had come to a deeper understanding of Tokugawa society. Rather, it reflected a changed perception of his patient's needs. When he wrote *Outline* in 1875, Japan was in need of an enlightened citizenry and his prescription was a massive infusion of the spirit of Western civilization. By 1892, Japan's civilization had advanced and a nascent citizenry was in place. What the Japanese needed, in Fukuzawa's view, was a realization that the new national assembly had Japanese, as well as Western, roots. Reconnecting with the past, even if the reconnection was shaky, would provide a basis for further progress. Though the two instances draw on history in diametrically opposite ways, each provided a rationale for action. The acuity and depth of each analysis was a result of this perception of immediate needs.

A Bird in Flight: The Question of Foreign Relations

Scholarly opinion generally regards *Outline* as Fukuzawa's finest work, the crowning achievement of his mature thought. I would agree, although I also have a high regard for several of his later works. But "maturity" should not be taken to mean that his thought in 1875 was in some sense finished or complete. To the contrary, it was very much in the middle of a transition between two rather different modal positions. The first modality was during the years just before and just after 1870, when Fukuzawa viewed the West as nonthreatening and accepted a philosophy of natural rights. This phase culminated in his translation of the chapter "Of the Absolute Rights of Individuals" from William Blackstone's *Commentaries on the Laws of England* and in the early chapters of *An Encouragement of Learning.* The second modality was just before and after 1880, though some signs of it appeared earlier. During this second period, he saw the West as a dire threat to Japan and flatly denied the idea of natural rights. *Outline* was written in the middle of the transition from the one to the other. The work was like a bird in flight.

To look first at foreign relations, the final chapter in *Outline*, "A Discussion of Our Country's Independence," is of critical importance. Fukuzawa began the chapter by reaffirming all that he had written earlier in the book about civilization being the long-term goal of mankind. It is "vast and noble," it encompasses "every endeavor of the human spirit." "When human knowledge and virtue reach their fullest development, our goals will be noble and timeless, and not limited to the piddling matter of one country's independence."

But then Fukuzawa reversed his position and stated that "at this stage of our national development," primacy must be given not to the advancement of civilization, but to Japan's independence.

In relations between nations in today's world, it is too early to speak of such noble and timeless goals. Anyone who does so is a foolish dreamer. Especially, when we look at Japan's situation at present, we are struck by its urgency and we find no leeway for other concerns. We must first ensure the continuing existence of Japan and of its people, and afterwards talk of civilization. If there is no country and no people, one cannot speak of Japanese civilization. This is why I narrow my argument and proclaim our country's independence as the sole goal of civilization.[58]

The emphasis on national independence in this passage does not come as a total surprise. In his earlier discussion of civilization, after equating the "national polity" with independence, he had written: "The only duty of Japanese at present is to preserve Japan's national

polity; to preserve the national polity will be to preserve national sovereignty." Still, to make civilization the means and independence the end
does seem to contradict the spirit of his earlier chapters. Was the final
chapter tacked on, we wonder, after the other chapters were written?
Especially puzzling is the timing of his argument. Why did he suddenly
in 1875 become concerned for Japan's national independence?

It is beyond the scope of this book to examine the complex nature of
Western imperialism in the middle of the nineteenth century. But it
seems fairly clear that the danger from the foreign powers was larger
in the 1850s and 1860s when Japan was weak and vulnerable. In the
1860s, numerous incidents occurred, including assassinations of Westerners and attacks on daimyo domains by Western warships. Mean-
while, the domains asserted their autonomy, the powerless Kyoto court
dabbled in politics, and the movement to "honor the emperor" and
"overthrow the bakufu" gathered strength. Bereft of support, the bakufu floundered and finally collapsed. In the face of such disarray, the
foreign powers, had they been so minded, had ample opportunities to
reduce Japanese sovereignty beyond the impositions already written
into the "unequal treaties."

During these years of peril, however, Fukuzawa's attention was narrowly focused on Japan's internal struggles, and not on the foreign
threat. In 1858, when he arrived in Edo as a scholar of Western Studies, he was already inclined to support the bakufu's open-the-country
policy and the treaties it had signed. Every aspect of his subsequent career, as noted earlier, depended on his Western expertise—his school,
travel abroad, job, and appointment as a direct retainer of the Tokugawa shogun. As a translator at the bakufu foreign ministry, he certainly had a detailed knowledge of the dispositions of the foreign powers, but his animus was wholly directed against the internal enemies of
the Tokugawa—the obstreperous domains that wanted to "expel the
barbarians." In an 1866 petition, he strongly advocated the subjugation
of one of those domains, Chōshū, and to this end he made the extraordinary suggestion that foreign troops be used to supplement Tokugawa
forces.

In comparison to the internal threat, Fukuzawa saw the foreign powers as somewhere off in the distance, an almost benign presence. They
interfered in Japan's politics only when their nationals were attacked or
when their treaty rights were thwarted, responses that he felt were only
to be expected. Fukuzawa's attitude toward the Western powers is re-

vealed in a letter to friends in 1863. Commenting on British newspaper reports about the British bombardment of Kagoshima that year, an act of retaliation that Fukuzawa felt was not entirely unjustified, he wrote: "The British do not take pleasure in arbitrarily resorting to arms and contravening the principles of Heaven."[59]

After 1869, Japan became more secure. Internal strife ended, and though sporadic samurai rebellions loomed large in people's minds, they were speedily suppressed. The new Meiji government upheld the treaties, encouraged Western learning, and adopted Western-style institutions. As former domains became prefectures, as a new national army was formed, and as daimyo and samurai were pensioned off, a more stable and unified society emerged.

Considering Japan's new stability, why did Fukuzawa become increasingly anxious about his nation's relations with the West? Why did he now worry about Japan's independence? Whatever the reasons, a rising concern for these questions can be traced through his writings. As early as 1869, in a long letter to a Nakatsu friend, he described his personal circumstances and the enormous changes occurring in Japan. But he also mentioned his concern for national independence and his scorn for foreigners who cared only for the profits from trade. "At this time our adversaries *(aite)* are the foreigners. In their relations with us, they have utter contempt for those with neither property nor learning. Can the contempt of these foreign outsiders make anyone born in Japan feel good?"[60]

A year later, his sense of foreigners as adversaries had become even more acute.

At present, our country has begun to trade with foreign nations. Some foreigners are dishonest, and for the sake of their own profit, wish to keep our country poor and our people ignorant. This being the case, those Japanese who advocate National Studies or Chinese Studies, who yearn for old ways and dislike the new, who through ignorance of the wider world fall into poverty and stupidity, are doing just what the foreigners want. They are playing into their hands. Today the only thing that foreigners worry about is whether we will master Western Studies.[61]

In 1873 and 1874, he wrote in *An Encouragement of Learning* that all nations, weak or strong, have equal rights. "Just as a sumo wrestler must not use his strength against an invalid, so must stronger nations respect the rights of the weak."[62] Fukuzawa believed that to ensure these rights is the duty of all, or at least, it should be. But, in fact, the equal rights of weaker nations were not being observed. India had been a great civilization, and Turkey, a great military empire. But now:

> India is a colony of Britain, and its people are like slaves of the British government. At present, the enterprise of Indians is to grow opium that poisons the Chinese. British merchants alone reap the profits from this trade in death. The government of Turkey is nominally independent, yet British and French merchants monopolize its commercial rights. Because of free trade, its production diminishes day by day . . . Its heroic warriors, constrained by poverty, become useless.[63]

As critical as he was of the imperial powers, Fukuzawa also found fault with India and Turkey. Countries are responsible for their own plight; India and Turkey, overly satisfied with conditions within their countries, had become complacent. They ought to have compared themselves to others and resolved to forge ahead. The lesson for Japan was clear.

He expressed similar feelings in a letter to Baba Tatsui (1850–1888) in 1874. Baba, a Keiō graduate studying in London, would later become a leader in the People's Rights Movement. "Although the military rebellions within Japan have now been suppressed, the turmoil in people's minds has not ended and may continue unabated for a time yet." The danger is that "given our present condition, we will be unable to withstand the impact of foreign relations, foreigners will daily violate our legal and commercial rights, and we may eventually find ourselves in a hopeless condition."[64]

> Japan's situation is truly difficult. To balance our foreign relations, an internal balance must be reached. To balance our internal affairs, our ignorance must be dispelled. If we attend to the internal first, it will be too late for the foreign. If we try to face up to the foreign, internal villains will interfere. If we think about this and ponder about that, nothing will get done. Still, the difficulty of the situation is no reason for inaction.[65]

By the time he wrote *Outline* in 1875, Fukuzawa's sense of crisis had deepened. He still identified the West with civilization; that had not changed.

> Recently, we have entered into relations with foreigners and have begun to compare their civilization to our own. In externals, the superiority of their technology and industrial arts is beyond discussion, but internally, too, the differences remain great. Western peoples are mentally active, self-disciplined, and well-ordered in their social relations. From the level of the national economy, down to the family and individual, in our present state, we Japanese cannot possibly compete. In a word, the Western nations are civilized and we as yet are not. Today, this has become completely clear, and there is no one who does not recognize the fact in his heart.[66]

But it was just because they were "civilized" and possessed the power that accompanies civilization that Westerners were dangerous. In *Outline*, Fukuzawa contrasted them with the traditional ruling elites, court nobles and samurai officials. Because of the imbalance of power, the old elites had inflicted suffering and humiliation, but even then, "they were Japanese" and could be dealt with.

> The cunning and ferocity of today's foreigners is incomparably greater than that of nobles or bakufu officials. They use their learning to dupe and their eloquence to deceive. They are fearless in battle and strong in warfare, and may be thought of as a vastly superior class of nobility who combine intelligence, eloquence, bravery, and strength. Should we, by any remote chance, become subject to their rule and constraints, their fine-grained cruelty will deprive us of the air we breathe and the people of Japan will die of suffocation. When we imagine this happening, our entire bodies shudder and our hair stands on end![67]

Fukuzawa also quoted a criticism of Commodore Perry and of foreigners in Japan that his close colleague Obata Tokujirō (1841–1905) had written. Obata, also a samurai from the Nakatsu domain, was six years Fukuzawa's junior. According to Obata, when Perry came to Ja-

pan, he had asked for trade, saying, "All men are brothers who live under the same sky and tread the same earth." Obata commented: "How
beautiful were his words, but how ugly his actions!" "What he meant
was 'we will kill anyone who does not trade with us.'" In Obata's opinion, the behavior of "arrogant" foreign merchants in Japanese cities
was no better. "They ride on horses and in carriages, forcing others to
avoid them." When there is a quarrel, "they hit and kick us, but our
cowardly, servile people lack the spirit to respond. Saying that nothing
can be done, they swallow their anger and do not take the foreigners
to court." Our people are weak, "like a young bride facing her mother-
in-law."[68]

In an unpublished memorandum written in the autumn of 1875,
Fukuzawa commented further on the disparity between words and actions in Christian civilization:

> Based on the teachings of Jesus, to love all mankind, to forgive
> them, and to act on their behalf is called the religion of brotherly
> love. In today's human affairs, to act for oneself, for one's wife,
> children, family, and country, while injuring others and benefiting
> oneself, might be called the religion of self-interest. It is self-
> evident that the tenets of these two religions are incompatible, and
> yet the peoples of Western countries, who at present call them-
> selves civilized, uphold and believe both creeds. Is it not wondrous
> that on Sundays, they shed tears as they listen to the scriptures ex-
> pounding the love of man, and on Mondays, convert to the creed
> of self-interest and act like demons? For one day they are like
> Buddha, for six days they are like demons; today the potato worm,
> tomorrow the butterfly. The cycle of their transformations goes
> on without limits. It is truly laughable.[69]

Fukuzawa touched on the same theme in *Outline*. The brotherhood
of man is an attractive ideal, but the real world is divided into competing nation-states. Private individuals of different nations may become
good friends, but "in relations between countries, only two things matter: In peace, goods are traded in a mutual struggle for profit; in war,
weapons are used to kill one another." From the viewpoint of religion,
this may be abhorrent, "but in the present state of civilization, it is un-
avoidable" and even has some benefits. Successful trade requires intel-

ligence, a cultivation of learning and the arts, and it is at the same time a reflection of national prosperity. Wars, too, are subject to multiple constraints and may be just and fought for honor. "It must be said that war is the technique for extending the rights of independent nations and that trade is evidence of national glory."[70]

Fukuzawa admitted that despite the treaties, Japan was still in relatively good condition:

> Foreigners came to our country only recently. To date, they have not inflicted any great harm, nor have they robbed us of our national honor. Because of this, the feelings of the people are not aroused. But those seriously concerned for the nation must widen their knowledge and comprehend the facts of world history.[71]

A look around the world revealed the danger of the foreign threat. Fukuzawa wrote of India as "a warning to Japan." There, the British practiced a cruel and heartless tyranny with no pretense at equality. In America, the white man had taken the country from its original inhabitants. In Persia, Siam, Luzon, and Java, similar patterns had emerged. And in the vast land of China, to date the white man had only encroached on the coast, but if the future may be imagined, "all of Imperial China will become nothing more than a garden for Europeans."[72]

> Where Europeans touch, land withers and plants and trees cease their growth. In extreme cases, entire populations have been wiped out. When these facts are understood, and when we bear in mind that our Japan is also a country of East Asia, then even if we have not yet been severely damaged in our foreign relations, we must fear future disasters.[73]

How should this "disease of foreign relations" be treated? After rejecting proposals by scholars of the National Studies, Confucian, and Christian camps, Fukuzawa presented his own solution: Japan should mobilize all of the resources of its existing civilization toward maintaining its independence, and at the same time, move forward toward a Western style of civilization. To underline the urgency of the matter, he sternly advised: "Every morning, Japanese worthy of the name of citizen (*kokumin taru mono*) should admonish each other to remain vigilant regarding foreign relations, and only then partake of breakfast."[74] During the years after 1875, Fukuzawa's fear of the danger of foreign aggression grew ever keener.

A Bird in Flight: The Question of Philosophy

A second feature in the transition between the two modalities was a shift in his philosophical assumptions, a shift in his worldview. During the late 1860s and into the 1870s, Fukuzawa was an optimist. He believed in progress; he believed in a higher human nature. Leaders may err, history has its ups and downs and never moves in a straight line, but as long as an immanent and beneficent nature is at work—almost as a substrate just beneath the surface of a less than perfect reality—all will turn out well. Nature and man's higher nature serve as a corrective, an invisible hand, always there to put things back on course. As knowledge advances and nature is better understood, as man learns to act in accord with his own true nature, progress is almost guaranteed.

A key element in his positive view of human nature was natural rights. In 1868, Fukuzawa translated the chapter titled "Individual Rights and Duties" in Burton's *Political Economy.* Two years later, he translated the chapter "Of the Absolute Rights of Individuals" in an abridged edition of Blackstone's *Commentaries on the Laws of England.* The best evidence that he accepted their ideas on human rights is contained in an epistle he wrote to friends in Nakatsu when he visited his old domain late in 1870. To appeal to the sensibilities of people schooled in Chinese Learning, Fukuzawa began with the Confucian idea that "man is the glory of creation" *(banbutsu no chō).* But then he reinterpreted the meaning of the term, explaining that it is true only when man "follows the way of heaven, cultivates virtue, broadens the experience and learning that make him human, and establishes his own independence and the livelihood of his family." He continued:

> Though Chinese and Japanese from ancient times have given it little heed, there exists in human nature *(ningen no tensei)* the way *(michi)* of independence and freedom *(jishu jiyū).* When one says "freedom," the word sounds like "selfishness" *(wagamama),* but that is not the case. Freedom means acting according to the dictates of one's own heart while not interfering with [the freedom of] others.[75]

In the mid-1870s, however, new ideas entered Japan and the popularity of the philosophy of natural rights weakened. Scholars read and translated John Stuart Mill, Herbert Spencer, and Henry Thomas Buckle. Buckle's *Civilization in England* was translated into Japanese in 1874, and beginning in 1875, was used as a text at Fukuzawa's Keiō School, along with writings by Mill. Buckle believed in progress but his approach to it was empirical, not metaphysical. Carmen Blacker cites a Keiō scholar who wrote: "When Buckle first appeared, the whole atmosphere at Keiō Gijuku suddenly changed. People ceased altogether to study the Bible."[76] Katō Hiroyuki (1836–1916), a leading advocate of "civilization and enlightenment" and later president of Tokyo Imperial University, abandoned his belief in natural rights during the late 1870s after reading Buckle, Darwin, and Spencer. In 1881, he published *New Theory of Human Rights (Jinken shinsetsu)* in which he repudiated his earlier belief in natural law. Among Japanese intellectuals, only those in the "People's Rights Movement," who needed natural rights to buttress their arguments, and some Christians, resisted this change in the intellectual climate.

Outline was written while this shift was under way, and as such, contains passages pointing in both directions. There are several passages that might have come from Fukuzawa's translation of Burton: "Human life is by nature suited for civilization; in all probability this is not accidental but results from the deep intent of the Creator (*zōbutsushu*)."[77] We find other passages that seem to assume a fixed human nature but argue that it was not properly understood in the past. Confucius, for example, taught the five human relationships (*gorin*) and assumed that they were a part of an innate human nature, a part of what humans receive from Heaven. Fukuzawa agreed that four of the five were so, but that the fifth, the "ruler-subject relationship, which in Japan and China had been viewed as inherent in human nature," did not stand up under empirical scrutiny.

Do not violate the true principles of things (*butsuri*) by rash conjectures. The ruler-subject relationship is a case in point. The relationship is one between one person and another. Though a principle (*jōri*) may be discerned therein, it is derived from the occasional existence of rulers and subjects in the world and does not mean that the relationship is inherent in human nature (*hito no sei*). In order to claim that it is a part of human nature, one would have

to show that in every country of the world, wherever there is a
person, there must be a ruler, and this, in fact, is not the case.
In all human societies there are parents and children, husbands
and wives, young and old, and friends: these four relationships
are what humans receive from heaven *(hito no tenpin)* and ought
to be described as a part of their nature. But the ruler-subject
relationship alone is not found in some countries of the world,
such as those in which representative government has been established.[78]

The ruler-subject relationship, he concluded, is not a part of nature.
This is merely one instance where the Chinese and Japanese had it
wrong and Europeans, with their deeper knowledge of the world, had
it right.

We also find passages that stress the difficulty of knowing what is
natural. At the opening of *Outline*, he addressed the question directly:

In the case of long-standing customs, it is almost impossible to
distinguish between what is natural *(tennen)* and what is man-
made *(jin'i)*. Among those principles that are considered natural,
some are merely customary. Among those that are recognized as
customary, some are natural. It must be admitted that a discussion
of civilization is difficult since it entails searching out true principles amid this confusion.[79]

A passage on equality raises the same difficulty. Fukuzawa noted that
the idea of equal rights *(jinmin no dōken* or *dōkenron)* had swept Japan
and that no one was speaking out against it. But he believed that the
idea was weak because it was not rooted in the daily lives of the people.
To illustrate the point, Fukuzawa cited the propensity of scholars to argue for equality within Japan while ignoring the inequality between
Japanese and foreigners. Throughout his discussion, which runs for
several pages, Fukuzawa seems to sidestep the question of whether
equality is, in fact, grounded in nature.[80]

The transitional character of *Outline* is thrown into sharp relief when
we examine his writings a few years later. In a collection of his essays
published in January 1878, Fukuzawa returned to the question of what
is natural:

The [statues of] Kannon of Asakusa and the Fudō of Narita are said to have miraculous powers and draw crowds of pilgrims. But why is it that so few believe in the Kannon and Fudō of lonely villages and out of the way places? . . . It is not the statues of the Buddhas they believe in, but rather, in other believers, and they make their pilgrimages accordingly.

Scholars are apt to speak of what is natural *(tenri jindō)*. They say that such and such is based on the principles of nature *(tenri)*, or that such and such is contrary to human nature *(jindō)*, as if these were fixed, unchanging, immovable principles that are true for all time, but in reality this is absurd.

Putting aside the distant past, even at present, what is viewed as natural varies from country to country, and it may change in the space of a few years. In Chinese and Japanese families, it is natural for the husband to be pompous and domineering. In the West, it is natural for the wife to be arrogant. A few years back, during the feudal era, it was natural for a vassal to give up his life for his daimyo; today it is natural for him to treat his [former] daimyo as an equal . . . What some writers refer to as natural is not a careful explication of the principles underlying their thought, but the prevailing opinion in their society by which they have been carried along. If public opinion holds that something is a true principle, they believe it; if public opinion holds that it is false, they doubt it . . . They do not seek that which is truly natural *(tenri jindō no hontai)* . . . They are not a whit different from those who believe in the Kannon of Asakusa or the Fudō of Narita . . . Scholars of my persuasion do not believe in what was called in both past and present a natural ethical order *(tenri jindō)*.[81]

In 1881, Fukuzawa further clarified his position in an essay titled "A Comment on the Times" *(Jiji shōgen)*. There he attacked outright the idea of natural law.

In human society there is a mixture of good and bad persons, just as there is a mixture of the sick and healthy. Originally, it was not man's nature to become sick. That he becomes so is due to malnutrition, to the spread of infectious disease, or to heredity. Yet under the prevailing conditions, it would not be a wise policy to abol-

ish medicine as a useless art on the grounds that man is naturally
without disease. It is better to wait until that time in the distant future when disease actually has disappeared. I cannot guarantee
that such a time will come. Thus, without realizing that bad persons as well as good are present in human society, to say that laws
are useless, and to tilt to one side and speak only of good human
nature *(tennenron)*, is like forgetting the sick and abolishing medicine. Laws are made for evil men, just as medicine is for the dis-
eased. Millions of years hereafter, when disease has vanished and
all men are good, laws and medicine may be abolished. In the
meantime, it is simply useless to speak of popular rights based on
nature *(tennen no minkenron)*; they are not worth discussing.[82]

What Fukuzawa wrote about philosophy had implications for his view
of foreign relations. He continued:

There are two ways of looking at the nature of relations between
the countries of the world—the ideal and the real. The ideal holds
that all of the peoples of the world . . . though different in their degree of civilization and enlightenment . . . are created equal and
are brothers in the eyes of God *(jōtei)* . . . At times, ignorant of this
great principle, they bear fearful weapons and slaughter their fellow men . . . yet as universal love gradually advances, as international law is drawn up and put into practice . . . the day will come
when the entire world will be at peace and war will have disappeared . . . At present, this ideal is espoused mainly by Western
ministers of Christianity or by persons enamored of this religion,
and it coincides to some extent with the idea that freedom is a natural right *(tennen no jiyūron)* . . .
    When we hear of this ideal, we cannot help but exclaim that it is
just and beautiful. But when we move away from the ideal and
look at the reality of international relations today, we find that the
two are shockingly different. Do nations . . . honor treaties? There
is not the slightest evidence that they do. When countries break
treaties . . . there are no courts to judge them. Therefore, whether
a treaty is honored or not . . . depends solely on the financial and
military powers of the countries involved . . . Money and soldiers
are not for the protection of existing principles; they are instruments to create principles where none exist.

Some idealists will no doubt sit and wait for the day when wars will end. But in my opinion, the Western nations grow ever stronger in the arts of war. In recent years, every country devises strange new weapons. Day by day they increase their standing armies. This is truly stupid and useless, yet if others work at being stupid, we must respond in kind. If others are violent, then we, too, must be violent . . . At the start of this essay I referred to the theory of man-made state rights (kokken) as the way of force (kendō) [in contrast to the way of virtue or seidō]. I am a follower of the way of force.[83]

Thus, by the end of the 1870s, the changes in Fukuzawa's views of foreign relations and philosophy—and we might think of these as two superimposed grids—had become mutually reinforcing. A critical view of the West had lent support to the idea that "money and soldiers . . . create principles where none exist," and a more somber view of nature had made the world of international relations seem less friendly. Fukuzawa now dismissed the philosophy of natural rights as the fatuous idealism of Christian ministers. He also consigned the law of nations, which he had earlier insisted on, to the dust heap of wishful thinking.

This is not to say that Fukuzawa had abandoned the idea of progress. He still believed that advances in human rationality and in the natural sciences would increase human control over the forces of nature, and that technology and invention would increase the wealth and wellbeing of society. "Civilization," as represented by Great Britain, was still his goal for Japan. But the metaphysical substrate that had given a rosy cast to his earlier conception of civilization was gone. Neither nature nor the West could be counted on to help. The future of Japan now depended wholly on the efforts and will of the Japanese.

Reflections

The Civilization and Enlightenment Movement

Western scholars usually speak of the civilization and enlightenment movement in Japan during the 1870s as the "Japanese Enlightenment." I have no quarrel with this. Many of the ideas that Japan took in from the West were nineteenth-century restatements of eighteenth-century ideas and had many points in common with the movement of that name in the West. But the exceptional nature and overarching importance of the movement in Japan must be kept firmly in mind. A simple comparison may help make the point.

In the West, the scientific revolution of the seventeenth century led to the Enlightenment of the eighteenth. Without Galileo and Newton, there would have been no John Locke or Adam Smith. One set of ideas inspired the other. The industrial revolution was less connected to these grand ideas, but in small ways it may also have inspired Enlightenment thinkers. The stage of "civilization" was seen as having industrial underpinnings. Watt patented his steam engine in 1769, just seven years before the *Wealth of Nations* was published in 1776.

In Japan the progression of events had a different order: the "enlightenment" or *kaika* movement came first, and the scientific and industrial revolutions followed. To put this more concretely, Japan had no scientific revolution in either the seventeenth or eighteenth century.

144

(Dutch Studies and herbology—*honzōgaku*—appeared, but too great a weight cannot be placed on their frail shoulders.) Nor did these centuries see an industrial revolution. (The thriving commercial economy of Edo and the development of local craft industries helped to prepare the way for what would come, but they did not presage a transition to machine industry.) Revolutionary changes began only in the mid-nineteenth century with the *kaika* movement, which was a response to the military, economic, and intellectual challenge of the West. And both the scientific revolution—if the Meiji embrace of science may be called that—and the industrial revolution were the products, in a sense, of "revolutionary" *kaika* (or *keimō*) thought.

This order of events suggests that the blossoming of *kaika* thought was not just a "movement" in the usual sense of the term. It was the intellectual and social expression of the convulsion that transformed Japanese society at mid-century. Fukuzawa's pivotal role during this era was to explain to his countrymen what was happening, what it meant, and what they must do. It is impossible to think of a Western thinker who played a similar role, since Europe never faced a comparable challenge from outside forces.

During the early years after the Meiji Restoration, Japan was singularly open to new ideas. The collapse of the Tokugawa government had called into question old values and institutions. The Japanese people anticipated great changes but had no clear picture of what the changes would be, or how their lives would be affected. Their hopes for the future were mingled with uncertainty and apprehension. Japan's new leaders, who had come to power almost overnight, were also uncertain as to how to proceed. The slogans they had used in their struggle against the bakufu—"Honor the Emperor," "Expel the Barbarians," "Overthrow the Bakufu"—were no longer of any use. They agreed on the need to centralize power in their own hands in the name of the emperor. They also agreed, as the Charter Oath of April 1868 put it, that Japan must "seek knowledge throughout the world," and by "world" they meant the West. But they lacked the detailed information needed to translate these vague general goals into concrete policies.

It was at this juncture that Fukuzawa's writings, which were already widely read, had their greatest influence. His 1868 translation of Burton's *Political Economy* and his two 1869 translations of Mitchell's descriptions of the stages gave clear depictions of the progress of nations from rude beginnings to the highest refinement. They provided an explanation for Japan's weakness in the face of Western nations. They presented the West as a text in which Japanese could read the lessons of its own future development. The first and third volumes of *Conditions in the West*, published in 1866 and 1870, were equally important. They filled out the picture of the West by furnishing detailed national histories and sketches of governmental, military, financial, and educational systems. These provided templates for programs of reform. Copies of *Conditions in the West* sold in the hundreds of thousands. Even today, well-thumbed copies turn up in country storehouses. Fukuzawa later downplayed the success of the work by saying that it was like the proverbial "bat in a village without birds."

The enlightenment movement began during the early 1870s and continued until the end of the decade. Some say it lasted until the "craze for Europeanization" flared and guttered out during the mid-1880s. After that, although Westernization continued within the new institutions created during the 1870s, the pace of change slackened, and the earlier monolithic image of the West was replaced by more differentiated and sophisticated views. The movement had multiple causes, not all of which consisted of ideas, and it took a variety of forms. It had no single underlying organization, but was rather an assortment of Westernizing tendencies within the society. We might distinguish three of its components as the popular, the intellectual, and the governmental.

The popular component is reflected vividly in contemporary woodblock prints: gaslights and horse-drawn streetcars on the Ginza, foreign soldiers parading while a foreign ship unloads at a wharf, hot air balloons, the red brick Tokyo railway station, primary school students studying world geography in a Western-style school building that overlooks a rice paddy. Food and fashions were a part of the popular response. Ladies wore bonnets and bustled gowns. Young dandies with Western-style haircuts sported watches with gold chains, carried Western umbrellas, and sat at tables eating *sukiyaki*, a new beef dish. "I wonder why we in Japan haven't eaten such a clean thing before?" remarked one character in Kanagaki Robun's satire *The Beefeater*.[1] Another enthusiast was satirized as "instantly loving everything he hears about the West." The ideas of civilization and enlightenment slowly percolated through much of Japan, but the scenes depicted in woodblock prints were mainly of the national capital.[2]

The second, intellectual component of the movement was exemplified by the Meiji Six Society (Meirokusha), which was founded in
1873 (the sixth year of the Meiji era). Its members, among them Fukuzawa, regularly held debates and wrote articles for the *Meiji Six Journal*
on the application of Western ideas to Japan. The range of the journal
was wide, and included such topics as the family, wives and concubines,
good mothers, prostitution, torture, the death penalty, earthquakes, the
new chemistry, brick buildings, liberty, parliaments, the balance of
trade, religion, and church and state in America. The articles discussed
how far Japan should go in adopting Western ideas, values, and institutions, and which were the most important to Japan's progress.[3]

Most members of the Meiji Six Society had backgrounds similar to
Fukuzawa. All were born during the 1830s and 1840s and had received
an early education in the Chinese classics. Most had studied Dutch
and gone on to become bakufu officials, translators, or educators. Unlike Fukuzawa, however, most had joined the new government. Mori
Arinori (1847–1889), who founded the society on his return from study
in the United States, held various diplomatic posts and became education minister in the first Itō Hirobumi cabinet of 1885. Katō Hiroyuki
(1836–1916), who early emphasized natural rights and later turned to
Social Darwinism and German state-centered thought, became president of Tokyo Imperial University and was active in the early Diet.
Nakamura Masanao (1832–1891) studied in England and translated *On
Liberty* by John Stuart Mill and *Self-Help* by Samuel Smiles. The latter
work, titled in Japanese *Success Stories in the West*, rivaled Fukuzawa's
works in popularity. Other important figures were Nishimura Shigeki,
Nishi Amane, Mitsukuri Shūhei, and Tsuda Mamichi.

Tsuda, who had studied law in the Netherlands, wrote an article for
the third issue of the *Journal* titled, "A Discussion of the Ways to Advance Enlightenment." The article was pessimistic in tone:

When Western learning (horizontal writing) entered our country
it was initially suppressed, but when [Perry's] American ships came
to Uraga, the orientation of the country changed and Western
learning spread with lightning speed. Today, whenever we open
our mouths, it is to speak of "enlightenment." However, those of
us who incessantly discuss enlightenment are, at best, only a few
hundred officials, scholars, and newspaper editors. Relative to our
huge population of 30 million, are we not but a tiny fraction? In

fact, our people still cling to old ways, and are for the most part deluded by ideas of hells and heavens, karmic causality, rewards and punishments, the five elements, and geomancy. Can such an ignorant people *(gumin)* even be called half-civilized?[4]

Tsuda did not exaggerate. Despite the popularity of things Western in the bigger cities, and despite the hundreds of thousands who read tracts by Fukuzawa and other advocates of Westernizing reforms, the number of those who actively propagated the new ideas was small. Persuading the Japanese majority to accept new ways was an uphill task for both the government and the pamphleteers of enlightenment.

At the same time, there is scattered evidence of a "readiness" for change on the part of the Japanese that would at least qualify Tsuda's assessment. Edward Morse, an American biologist who taught at Tokyo Imperial University during the late 1870s, agreed with Tsuda regarding the prevalence of superstition, but he also spoke of his students as "mostly rationalists" who were "greedy to learn," and of his own "delight" in explaining Darwinian theory to students whose minds were not clouded by "theological prejudice."[5] Irokawa Daikichi has described the vitality of local responses to the writings of Fukuzawa and others, and focused on a group of villagers who were moved to write their own constitution for Japan.[6] Maruyama Masao cites the townspeople of Ōmiya in Shizuoka prefecture who began an "Enlightenment Society." Its goal was "to gather together newspapers and translations, debate the trends of the times, and discuss how to expand learning in order to advance toward enlightenment." The society met on the fifteenth of every month, and by the end of 1873, the original thirty members had grown to about a hundred.[7] Had their seed fallen on barren ground, the efforts of the Meirokusha pamphleteers would have come to naught.

The third component of the enlightenment movement was the Meiji government. Progressive officials planned and implemented a variety of Westernizing policies: stronger support for the treaties; the separation of legislative, executive, and judicial offices; the formation of a modern army and navy, a central governmental mint, and a postal system; as well as direct investments to establish a nationwide telegraph system, new ports, railroads, and the so-called model industries. The list could go on and on.

Itō Hirobumi was a key figure in these actions. Born in the Chōshū

domain in 1841, his family was at the very bottom of the samurai hier-
archy, but he attended, like many future Restoration leaders, the school
of the radical Confucian Yoshida Shōin. In 1866, during a civil war
in Chōshū, he commanded a troop of sumo wrestlers in battles against
the regular units of the domain's conservative government. He was also
a military commander during the Restoration wars. After the wars,
he entered the new government, rose quickly within its ranks, and in
1881, emerged as the single most powerful political figure in Japan. He
is generally regarded as the father, if not the author, of the 1889 Meiji
constitution. In 1900, Itō founded the Seiyūkai, the political party that
would dominate Diet politics for almost two decades.

In 1899, Itō delivered two speeches that give us an inkling of the
lasting influence exerted by civilization and enlightenment thought at
the highest levels of government. The speeches were representative of
dozens he gave during the late 1890s, but they are of particular interest
to us because of the extent to which they mirror Fukuzawa's ideas in the
early 1870s. In the first speech, delivered to middle school students in
Yamaguchi, Itō defined Japan's progress in terms of the ideal of "civilization," for which he took Europe as the model.

[From the time of the Restoration] to the present day, Japan has
taken civilization *(bunmei)* as its goal and has adopted the learning
(gakujutsu) of Europe. Yet, because we have had little time and because Japan's learning before the Restoration was so very different,
our progress has not yet made us equal to the countries of Europe
and America. We must, therefore, plan for even greater advancement, and our advancing scholarship *(gakugyō)* must necessarily be
applied to the actual problems of our society. When we look at the
condition of the civilized nations of the world, we note that their
recent progress has been truly remarkable, and that every one of
the various enterprises developed in their society has its basis in
learning.

The second speech, delivered only a few days later, contrasted barbarous and civilized states, and resoundingly affirmed that civilized behavior called for the recognition of "equal rights" between nations.

Japan's national policy of "opening the country" is not solely a
matter of opening the country [to foreign relations]. Many coun-

tries in the world at large [are open but] still continue to practice barbarous customs and are unable to reform and modify them so as to advance to the level of civilization. These countries are not admitted to the ranks of civilized nations but are dealt with as barbarians. From the start, the goal of our national policy has been to open ourselves to civilization, to become a nation of the world, and to join the company of the civilized countries of Europe and America *(bunmei no chii o shimuru Ōbei shokoku)*. To "enter the company" means to "become a member of the group." We must consider carefully the rights and duties this entails. Civilized nations uphold certain rights *(tsūgi)*; to do so is a requirement for acceptance to their ranks. In general, the countries of East Asia, including China and Japan, are prone to despise what is foreign while holding themselves in high esteem. But when relating to others in accord with the rights of civilization, each must practice the same courtesies, neither despising the other and honoring self, nor despising self and honoring the other. Independent countries must relate to one another as equals, possessed of the same rights and duties. These are spelled out in detail in what is called international law.[8]

Itō was an astute and articulate statesman. His ideas nevertheless strike us as a color-by-the-numbers version of the intricate tapestry of Fukuzawa's thought. John Maynard Keynes once observed that "practical men, who believe themselves to be quite exempt from any intellectual influences, are usually the slaves of some defunct economist." If we substitute "thinker" for "defunct economist," his observation could well apply to Itō.

Civilization and Enlightenment as Ideology

Itō's speeches raise another consideration: the extent to which "civilization and enlightenment" became an ideology for change during the early Meiji years.

In the West, the acceptance of the schema of stages carried with it no mandate for change. Western "civilization" was the peak of human progress, at least for the time being, from which even the best-intentioned writers could look down on the less fortunate peoples of the world. Burton and Mitchell may have been less self-congratulatory than Guizot, but they shared his complacency. The West, of which they were a part, was the most advanced area in the world; further progress, they believed, would come as a matter of course since progress was built into human nature. Strenuous efforts were not needed.

Fukuzawa and other Meiji thinkers stood on a lower elevation. Looking up, they saw the West leading and Japan lagging behind. Japan's government, Fukuzawa wrote, was autocratic *(senseiteki)*, its military weak, its economy backward, and it had few welfare institutions. Furthermore, it had barely scratched the surface of the great body of learning that Western scholars had built up. As noted earlier, in Fukuzawa's view, the only thing the Japanese had to brag about was their country's scenery. The perceived gap between the West and Japan led to a tremendous leverage for change. It was because *bunmei kaika* conceptualized this gap that it became an ideology for catching up with the West.[9]

In 1965, the economic historian Alexander Gerschenkron wrote an essay titled "Backwardness in Historical Perspective." In it, he discussed France, Germany, and Russia, the second wave of nations to industrialize in Europe. While the essay dealt primarily with economics, it also touched on the critical role of ideas:

> To break through the barriers of stagnation in a backward country, to ignite the imaginations of men, and to place their energies in the service of economic development, a stronger medicine is needed than the promise of better allocation of resources or even of the lower price of bread . . . Even the businessman . . . needs a more powerful stimulus than the prospect of higher profits. What is needed to remove the mountains of routine and prejudice is faith—faith, in the words of Saint-Simon, that the golden age lies not behind but ahead of mankind.[10]

In France, industrialization required a shift in banking philosophy. The new philosophy or faith, Gerschenkron argued, came from Saint-Simon's vision of the role of banks in an ideal industrial society. The shift away from commercial banking to industrial banking was implemented by the directors of Crédit Mobilier, who took Saint-Simon to heart. In Germany, comparable doctrines that prepared the way for industry came from Friedrich List, who adapted the teachings of Saint-Simon to fit German conditions. In Russia during the 1890s, it was Marxism, with its iron law of historical development, that convinced leaders of the inevitability and desirability of industry. Gerschenkron explained why Marxism was needed:

> In conditions of Russian "absolute backwardness," again, a much more powerful ideology was required to grease the intellectual and emotional wheels of industrialization than either in France or Germany. The institutional gradations of backwardness seem to find their counterparts in men's thinking about backwardness and the way in which it can be abolished.[11]

In sum, France was the most developed to start with, so it needed only a small ideological change—a sanction for a new kind of banking. In backward Russia, a tougher ideology and stronger state action was needed to offset the weakness of private institutions. In terms of this spectrum, nineteenth-century Japan was closer to Russia than to France. It needed far more than new banks. It required a blanket sanction to overhaul the entire society. "Civilization and enlightenment," with its optimistic faith in a golden future, was an ideology singularly appropriate to Japan's level of development.

But should the Gerschenkron model be applied to non-European countries? In his essay, Gerschenkron wrote only of fairly advanced countries with European traditions. (In calling them "backward," he simply meant that they lagged behind England.) He assumed that these countries, including Russia, possessed a common intellectual infrastructure of newspapers, journals, schools, universities, and publishing houses. He further assumed that this infrastructure would nurture thinkers who would respond to the challenge of industrialization in terms of their nation's "gradation of backwardness." But in the nineteenth century, most of the world was not on a European continuum. Most countries lacked such an infrastructure and lacked thinkers who could respond to the challenge. Outside of Europe, in fact, there existed an inverse ratio between the "gradations of backwardness" and the appropriate "counterparts in thought."

In this respect, Japan's readiness was remarkable. It was non-

European, yet it had a sufficient intellectual infrastructure to produce
thinkers like Fukuzawa who could respond to the Western challenge.
Part of the challenge was industrial. During the 1870s, exhortations
such as "encourage production and stimulate industry" *(shokusan kōgyō)*
and "enrich the country and strengthen the military" *(fukoku kyōhei)*
were used as slogans. But political goals were just as important. In *Outline*, Fukuzawa was not telling the Japanese to adopt Western institutions in order to enrich the country. His goals were national independence and progress to a Western level of "civilization." Western
economic institutions were as much an instrumentality as a goal. Itō,
too, though a determined champion of economic growth, was obviously concerned with Japan's standing among nations.

The magnitude of changes brought about by these ideas can only be
called revolutionary. Banks replaced moneylenders, or rather, banks
were created where none had existed before. Tokugawa handicraft industries gave way to government "model industries" that trained workers and managers, and these in turn gave way to the nongovernmental
cotton mills and new heavy industries of the 1890s. Modern military
forces replaced domain armies. The early Meiji Dajōkan, a European-
style government using the nomenclature of ancient Japanese institutions, replaced the elaborate offices and vested interests of the Tokugawa bakufu, and in turn was replaced by a cabinet system and national
assembly. Confucian academies gave way to European-style universities, with faculties trained in Europe and the United States. Each new
venture had its own set of ideas to explain its operations. But behind
such specific ideas was "civilization and enlightenment," the broad vision of a better society that had been realized in the West.

Erwin Baelz, a German doctor who lived in Japan during these years
of transformation, wrote:

Betwixt night and morning . . . and with one great leap, Japan is
trying to traverse the stages of five centuries of European development, and to assimilate in the twinkling of an eye all the latest
achievements of Western civilization. The country is thus under-
going an immense cultural revolution—for the term "evolution" is
inapplicable to a change so rapid and so fundamental. I feel myself
lucky to be an eyewitness of so interesting an experiment.[12]

Issues of Interpretation

Early in *Outline*, as a groundwork for his introduction of Buckle's statistics on murder and marriage, Fukuzawa wrote of the difficulty of comprehending the mental states of individuals.[13]

> The workings of the human heart are wonderfully complex; they differ from morning to evening and from night to day. Today's moral gentleman *(kunshi)* may be tomorrow's man of small virtue *(shōjin)*; this year's enemy may be next year's friend. Like phantoms or magic spirits, human transformations are beyond understanding or measurement. That the hearts of outsiders cannot be apprehended goes without saying, but even between husbands and wives and parents and children, changes of the heart cannot be measured. Nor is it family alone; we cannot even manage changes within our own hearts.[14]

To illustrate his point, Fukuzawa wrote of Hideyoshi, the unifier of late-sixteenth-century Japan. Hideyoshi began life as Tōkichi, a poor village boy who stole six gold *ryō* from his master to make a start in the world. He became a warrior, then a vassal in the service of the warlord Oda Nobunaga, and after he had advanced in rank, he took the name of Hashiba Hideyoshi. He eventually became a general, took the name of Toyotomi Hideyoshi, and after a series of unforeseen events, he became the Taikō or overlord of all Japan.

> When this person looked back from his position as Taikō and recalled what he had been like when he stole the six *ryō*, he must have felt that all the accomplishments of his life had happened by chance, as if he had entered a dream within a dream.
>
> When he was Tōkichi, he had the mind *(kokoro)* of Tōkichi; when he was Hashiba, the mind of Hashiba; and when he attained the position of Taikō, he naturally had the mind of the Taikō. The three stages of his life were not the same. His mental processes at each stage differed, and if one were to discuss these processes in greater detail, a thousand or even ten thousand changes might be discerned.[15]

But scholars, Fukuzawa added, "do not understand this." "They judge his entire life by his words and deeds as the Taikō." They speak of his "prodigious feats" while still a child, and "even cite the auspicious omens that preceded his birth."

One is tempted to think that Fukuzawa was reviewing his own life when he wrote of Hideyoshi. As the boy Yukichi, Fukuzawa had been poor, fatherless, and of low status in the castletown society of Nakatsu. He left his domain, became a student of Dutch, and in rapid succession, a teacher, bakufu official, direct retainer of the shogun, translator, and author. (Eventually Fukuzawa became known as "the sage of Mita"— the Taikō of Meiji intellectual life.) The twenty-year-old Yukichi who left Nakatsu in 1855 could never have imagined the transformations that lay before him.

In writing of Fukuzawa's early life, scholars today do not seek out auspicious omens or prodigious boyhood feats. But they still face the problem raised earlier—the difficulty of figuring out the workings of Fukuzawa's heart and of pinpointing exactly when, and why, changes occurred. It is easier to speak of his thought, and even that is only dimly perceived during his formative years.

Consider his early education. As a youth in Nakatsu, Fukuzawa became, like others of his class, a "Confucian." To be sure, he was not a Confucian scholar. He was a samurai youth inducted into the world beyond family and boyhood through the reading of the Confucian classics and Chinese histories. In his domain there was no alternative course of study. As it was, Confucian philosophy did not leave an indelible imprint on his mind—in the way that a religious education might have—but some of his lifelong intellectual orientations toward history and natural philosophy seem to have begun during these early years.

When did Fukuzawa abandon the Confucian teachings of his youth? In his autobiography, written forty years after the fact, he says it was during his Osaka years when he studied Dutch medicine. "Chinese medicine was our enemy and our dislike for the medicine extended to Confucianism; we felt that everything Chinese should be driven from Japan." This is credible. The elementary chemistry experiments that he performed at the Ogata school—making ammonium chloride or sulfuric acid—may have led him to reject the Confucian doctrine of yin-yang and the five elements, and this, in turn, may have raised some doubts about the entire Confucian philosophy. Later in life he frequently used yin-yang and the five elements to criticize the entire corpus of Confucian teachings. Yet the curriculum at the Ogata school was narrowly linguistic and medical, with only a dollop of the most basic science. These were not substitutes for the history and philosophy he had imbibed as a youth. Anatomy may have pushed history to the back of his mind, but it is hard to think of it as a replacement. It was not until the second half of the 1860s that he had mastered enough Western history and natural philosophy to replace the Confucianism of his youth. And even then, a careful reading of his translation of Burton's *Political Economy* reveals a few subterranean influences that might be called "Confucian." But any interpretation of these early years must be conjecture, for there are few historical sources about Fukuzawa that date from the 1850s.

Similarly, it is difficult to fathom the "workings of his heart" during the 1860s, and to weigh the influence of one factor against another. Despite the greater availability of historical materials, changes in Fukuzawa's life came so fast and thick that they are difficult to disentangle. Consider the simple question of why he began writing *Conditions in the West*, the work that profoundly changed his life. Was it spurred by his successful publication of a Cantonese-English phrasebook that he had bought in San Francisco in 1860 and to which he added Japanese readings? Was it inspired by his experience of travel abroad, by what he saw and heard in San Francisco in 1860, and then in Europe in 1862? Did his contributions to the official report of the bakufu mission in Europe in 1862—the first time he synthesized materials into a coherent narrative—lead him to take this step? Or was it his precise translations of diplomatic documents at the bakufu foreign office that gave him confidence as a translator as well as a perspective on Japan's relations with Western nations? Were his translations of Yokohama English-language papers that he distributed to officials in Edo the catalyst? Or did the stimulus come from the works he had read during the early 1860s, when he had turned to the study of English? And finally, when we ponder the workings of his heart, we must also ask why he was not content to sit back and enjoy the enormous increase in status that his bakufu job conferred. More than most of his fellow scholars, Fukuzawa seems to have possessed the restlessness, striving, and disposition for improving his condition that the Scots saw as an intrinsic part of human nature.

Whatever may be said about the earlier workings of his heart, Fukuzawa's life became more settled during the 1870s and, consequently, his
thought easier to grasp. He wrote books that were not translations and
wrote far more letters, an amazing number of which have survived and
are included in his *Collected Works*. One item of particular relevance to
his thinking about civilization was his *Plan for Theories of Civilization
(Bunmeiron puran)*, dated February 8, 1874. The document was discovered, or rediscovered, in 1991, wadded up behind a drawer in a wooden
chest given to Keiō University by Fukuzawa's family. It is brief and
written in short sentences as if he were itemizing points he intended to
make. It clearly conveys the state of his thought a year before the *Outline* was written.

Some elements of the *Plan* perfectly match those in *Outline*. The
Plan begins with a summation of the first chapter of the projected
book:

> The West is more civilized than Japan. Japan is more civilized
> than the Ainu lands, and that is all there is to say about the matter.
> In the future, as intelligence advances further, the present West
> may conceivably be regarded as barbarous. But if discussed in
> terms of intelligence in the world today, the civilization of the
> West is the highest.[16]

It concludes with the statement that civilization and enlightenment
must be Japan's goal and that the West must be accepted as the standard of judgment.

The *Plan*, however, contains no discussion of the schema of stages
and no elaboration of the spirit of civilization—whereas in *Outline*,
these followed immediately after the discussion of relativity. Did Fukuzawa have the stages so clearly in mind from his earlier translations that
he felt no need to include them in his notes? Also, since the *Plan* makes
no mention of Guizot's history, we assume that he read it after drawing
up the *Plan*.[17]

Buckle's ideas are prominent in the *Plan*, which leads us to believe
that Fukuzawa may have just read the early chapters of his *History of
Civilization in England*. The *Plan* defines civilization as "the advance of
knowledge *(chie)* and virtue *(tokugi)*," and it goes on to state: "Evil
in the world will not be vanquished by moral admonishments; virtue

(toku) is of little avail but intelligence *(chi)* has a far reaching influence. To speak of changes brought about by the emperor's virtue is empty prattle." Additional points made in the *Plan* are corollaries of these propositions.[18]

The *Plan* conspicuously lacks any discussion of national independence, though Fukuzawa saw fit to criticize the behavior of British merchants in Japan. "It is extremely difficult to counter the misbehavior *(ranbō)* of the British." "Until Japanese become their equal in knowledge," Japan should employ a "protective system." (Fukuzawa uses the English term.) "Who says that the British are benevolent *(go-shōnin)?* As far as business is concerned, they may be called demons. There is the scholar Adam Smith, but these British officials are not his disciples."[19] The *Plan*, however, does not touch on the hypocrisy of Christians or on the depredations of Western imperialism, which were important themes in *Outline*. These omissions suggest that the last chapter of *Outline*, in which independence is stressed as Japan's paramount goal, was added late in the writing process.

A final interesting difference is that, in *Outline*, Fukuzawa wrote to persuade. He addressed his intellectual foes, the scholars of Confucian and National Studies, not as enemies, but as misguided friends who would be open to reasonable argument. In contrast, he wrote the *Plan* for himself. It contains only the bare bones of his thought. His comments, accordingly, are blunt and unsparing. For example: "Until now, learning in Japan has been stupid. The Confucian classics are either guidebooks for slaves or instructions for the rearing of slaves. People are what their learning makes them."[20]

In all of Japan, the quantity of intelligence and virtue is small. As proof of this, we have made no inventions. Scholarship *(gakumon)* is merely a matter of words on a page, and the practical arts *(gigei)* are the products of happenstance. We have murderers and thieves; the number of criminals is incomparably greater than in Western countries. Especially lamentable is the widespread superstition *(wakudeki)* and the lack of daring and courage . . . Unless we rid ourselves of the false belief *(wakudeki)* in yin and yang and the five elements, we will be unable to understand the workings of nature. Unless we rid ourselves of the delusion *(wakudeki)* that some are high and noble and others low and base, we will be unable to un-

derstand human nature. Our lack of science and invention is a
consequence of such beliefs. Our failure to establish industries and
our errors in historical understanding also result from this . . . In
our present condition (*jisei*), it stands to reason that such failures
and errors will arise.[21]

It would be nice to know, of course, whether this was his first and only
plan, or his third, and whether it was followed by other plans closer to
the content of the finished book. But it is fortunate that one, at least,
has survived.

Another problem, for me at least, is the juxtaposition in Fukuzawa's
thought of patriotism and iconoclasm. (The iconoclasm need not necessarily be related to the childhood acts he describes in his autobiography, such as putting a tablet from the household shrine into the toilet,
or substituting one stone for another at an Inari shrine.) That he was a
patriot is beyond question: a profound concern for Japan's well-being,
independence, progress, and international standing permeates his mature writings. But he also was willing to abandon any traditional value
or practice that did not stand the test of reason or that interfered with
Japan's advance toward civilization. He seems not to have set aside as
sacrosanct any core of Japanese culture that had to be protected at all
costs. Is this not a strange sort of patriotism? Of course, in developing
nations, nationalism often becomes a substitute for an abandoned tradition. Perhaps Fukuzawa can be viewed broadly in such terms. But it
must be kept in mind that his "nationalism" was highly self-critical and
defined by what he perceived as the universalism of "civilization."

It is easy to overlook Fukuzawa's iconoclasm since he shared it to a
considerable extent with other thinkers of the early Meiji era. I was
made keenly aware of this when I read Raouf Abbas Hamed's *The
Japanese and Egyptian Enlightenment*. Hamed compares Fukuzawa with
Rifaʿah al-Tahtawi (1801–1873), a nineteenth-century Egyptian
thinker and reformer. Tahtawi had a more sustained contact with the
West than Fukuzawa: he spent five years in Paris (from 1826 to 1831)
and was fluent in French; in 1836 he became the head of a new School
of Languages in Cairo, and in 1841 he was put in charge of a translation bureau. He read Guizot, Rousseau, Robertson, and Montesquieu,
and he used stage theory in his writings. But in using it, he hedged or
compromised, as Fukuzawa did not. As an example of the first stage of

civilization, Tahtawi cited the people of the Sudan, who engage in hunting and primitive cultivation. For the second pastoral stage, he cited the Bedouin. But in writing of the highest stage, he included Egypt, Syria, Turkey, Persia, and Morocco, along with Europe and the United States. Had Fukuzawa, in the same manner, included Japan, China, and Korea among the ranks of "civilized" nations, all of the leverage for change he gained by stressing the gap between half-civilized and civilized would have been lost. Tahtawi further insisted that any change in basic human relations had to be compatible with Islamic law—with the Sha'riah. It was as if Fukuzawa had firmly advocated changes in a European direction—excepting those not compatible with the teachings of Confucius.[22]

Culture, Ideas, and the Self

A further insight into Fukuzawa's thought and feelings is afforded by his preface to *Outline*. He wrote this four-page passage in March 1875, after the book was finished. In the book itself, his focus was on the gap between Western and Japanese civilizations and his prescription for overcoming this. In the preface, he posed a slightly different question: What was the nature of the Western impact on Japan? In answering this, he seems to be describing the influence of the West on himself, and then to project his own feelings and thoughts onto Japan.

One feature of Japan's confrontation with the West was cultural. Within the West itself, Fukuzawa notes, the ideas that accompanied the rise of "civilization" were new and upsetting when first propounded: "They startled people's ears and eyes." But even so, they were not totally new in that they "arose from the same elements" (*dōitsu no genso*) as the old. During "the more than a thousand years of Western history (*enkaku*)" since the fall of Rome, there had been a continuous development in which "the surviving works (*ibutsu*) of earlier thinkers (*senjin*) were transmitted and improved (*sessa takuma*)."

> Comparing this [continuity] to the circumstances in our country today, the same logic does not apply. For our civilization, it [the arrival of the new ideas] is like fire turning to water, or like a shift from nonbeing to being. The suddenness of the change is such that it cannot be called a linear development; it is closer to a new

creation. It stands to reason that Western theories are extremely difficult to comprehend.[23]

Fukuzawa could have used the schema of stages to explain Japan's difficulty in taking in the new ideas. Instead, he talked of intellectual tradition. The specific term he used was *genso*, or element. Guizot had written in his history of the elements (he also calls them "principles" and "developments") that had contributed to European civilization. Fukuzawa started using "element" after he read Guizot. But in this passage, Fukuzawa seems to be using *genso* to mean "cultural element," which is slightly different from what Guizot meant by the term.[24]

Fukuzawa made the same cultural distinction in a second argument, where he contrasted the influence of Chinese ideas on Japan in the seventh century with the effect of Western ideas in the nineteenth. In the past, he wrote, Japan "frequently had upheavals and regime changes," but only twice did events occur that "penetrated deep into the inner recesses of men's hearts and aroused a profound response *(kandō)*." The first was in "ancient times when Buddhist and Confucian teachings were transmitted from China." The second was during Japan's recent encounter with the West. The teachings from China he characterized as "new but *not* strange," while those from the West were "new *and* strange." The Chinese teachings were not strange because "Asian cultural elements" *(Ajiya no genso)* were transmitted from one Asian country to another. The Chinese elements differed from those of Japan only in their "fineness or subtlety." (He did not define "Asian" or say what Chinese and Japanese elements had in common.) The elements entering from the West were strange because they were "non-Asian" and had followed a "different developmental track" *(hatsuiku o koto ni shi)*. Thus vis-à-vis Japan, the civilization of the West was distinctly "other" *(tokushu ibetsu)*.[25]

Fukuzawa used a variety of metaphors to express the "otherness" that he himself had experienced in the course of his studies and travels. Several have already been noted: "It was as if the deaf and blind . . . heard sounds and saw colors." It was "like a shift from nonbeing to being." But there were others: It was like "the hottest fire plunging into the coldest water." "It not merely caused waves on the surface of men's minds but penetrated to the bottom of their innermost being and stirred up a great turbulence *(tenpuku kaisen no daisōran)*." Or again:

"Only after the Americans arrived in the 1850s and treaties and trade began, did Japanese realize that the West actually existed and that its civilization was so hugely different *(ibetsu)* from their own. They were astounded and a tumult *(sōran)* arose in their hearts."[26]

The West was "strange" or "other," but Fukuzawa did not find it "alien." This is a critical distinction. He felt that the West had arrived at a deeper and more universal understanding of nature and human nature. Adam Smith's principles of economics explained the behavior of shopkeepers in Edo just as well as they did that of their counterparts in London. The theories of civilization propounded by Burton, Guizot, and Buckle enabled Japan to see its own history in a new and more revealing light. The rights of freedom and equality, especially as they pertain to women, Fukuzawa felt, had long been neglected in East Asia, but since they inhere in human nature, they would be realized as Japan progressed toward "civilization." Fukuzawa found these ideas liberating, and making them his own, restated them forcefully in terms his countrymen could easily grasp. Consider the following passage on the equality of women from his 1870 epistle to Nakatsu:

> The foundation of morality is the husband and wife. Parents and children, brothers and sisters, come afterwards. At the very beginning, when heaven gave rise to human beings, there must have been one man and one woman. Though tens of millions of years have passed since then, the ratio remains the same. Men and women stand equally as individuals between heaven and earth; there is no reason to weigh them differently. In the past and at present Chinese and Japanese custom permit one man to take several women as wives or concubines, and women are treated like servants or wrongdoers, yet no one feels shame. Is this not despicable!
>
> If a man has the right to wed two women, then it stands to reason that a woman may possess two men. Let me ask you men of Japan, if your wife loved another, and your home had one wife and two husbands, could you tolerate the situation?[27]

As a youth, or even as a young man in 1858, Fukuzawa could not have conceived of such ideas. When he wrote of Western ideas stirring up "a turbulence in the innermost being" of the Japanese, he is projecting the radical transformation that he had experienced within himself.

As we read the Preface to *Outline*, we imagine Fukuzawa sitting in his study at Mita. He has completed the chapters and is satisfied with the work. He asks himself, "What can I say in this preface that will present the book to my readers in an attractive light?" One thing he did was to make several modest disclaimers like those he had voiced in his introduction to *Conditions in the West*. Apologizing for the roughness of his arguments and his many errors, he predicted that future scholars would produce better interpretations of civilization. If now and then there were useful ideas in his book, they were not his own but the thought of others that he had digested.

This disclaimer notwithstanding, Fukuzawa went on to suggest that the book offered one perspective that his readers were unlikely to find in the writings of any Western thinker. Earlier, he had argued that Japan's cultural tradition created difficulties for the understanding of new and strange ideas. Now he argued that in one singular respect that very same tradition had given Japanese scholars of his generation a "windfall advantage" that Western scholars could not match.

> Ever since the opening of Japan, Japanese scholars have applied themselves to Western Learning, and though their studies have so far been crude and limited, they have gleaned some idea of Western civilization. Yet barely twenty years earlier, those same scholars were immersed in a purely Japanese civilization *(junzentaru Nihon no bunmei)*, which they not only observed but personally experienced in their lives. Because of this, when discussing the past, they are less likely to resort to vague conjectures. They can directly use their own experience to shed light on [the early stages of] Western civilization. In this single regard, our scholars, with their experience, will prove more reliable than Western scholars, who attempt to conjecture about conditions in other lands from within the confines of their already advanced civilization. The advantage of which I speak derives wholly from the unique experience of present-day scholars, an experience that will never come again once this present generation is gone. Consequently, it must be said that the present offers a uniquely valuable opportunity.
>
> Consider for a moment that today's scholars of the West were but a few years ago, all students of Chinese learning, all adherents of Shinto and Buddhism, all feudal warriors or people living within the feudal system. It is just as if a person had led two lives in a sin-

gle body, or as if a single person possessed two bodies. What insights may be gained when they examine their earlier lives in the light of their very different experience of Western civilization! Their arguments will surely be reliable.[28]

When Fukuzawa wrote of the "experience" of his "generation of scholars," he was referring primarily to their stage of civilization. Japanese can better understand other less developed countries because, until recently at least, they were at the same stage. They shared with other peoples the features common to that stage. In Fukuzawa's words, we hear a distant echo of Robertson's contention that each stage is much the same the world around, and that "a tribe of savages on the banks of the Danube must nearly resemble one upon the plains washed by the Mississippi." But within the stage, Fukuzawa recognizes cultural distinctiveness. It is obvious that other members of the set of "half civilized societies" cannot be called "purely Japanese."

The passage also seems to reflect, if only slightly, the ambivalence that was so evident in the chapters of *Outline*. Western scholars who wrote on civilization never imagined less developed lands as actors on the international stage. They never put themselves in the position of the inhabitants of less developed lands. They never considered the political consequences of the awareness of being less developed. In contrast, Fukuzawa's writings were suffused with such a consciousness. He stood several rungs down on the ladder of progress, and looking up, saw the "enlightened" West, which he admired almost as much as the West admired itself. But he also observed the arrogance of its representatives in Japan, the Western imperialism that rode roughshod over human and national rights, and the potential threat to Japan that caused whatever "it touches to wither and trees to die." Fukuzawa saw the theory of stages from a perspective not found in the writings of any Western writer on civilization.

The same passage also affords us a glimpse of Fukuzawa, the scholar and self-made man. He went from a boyhood in the backwater of Nakatsu to become an official in the Tokugawa government only to see his career collapse about him. He then picked himself up and began a new life as an independent writer and thinker in Meiji Japan. He had lived two distinct lives in one body. When he wrote *Outline* in 1875, he was at the peak of his powers and successful beyond all expectations.

He had laid the foundations for what would be a long and vigorous career, and his thought was still developing. But he was also at a turning point in his life. He looked back at the distance he had traveled and reflected on what it meant. Could he have thought, like Hideyoshi, that his life was a dream within a dream?

Notes
Bibliography
Illustration Sources and Credits
Index

Notes

Works frequently cited in the notes have been identified with the following abbreviations:

FZS *Fukuzawa Yukichi zenshū.* Tokyo, 1969–1971.

PE John Hill Burton, *Political Economy for Use in Schools, and for Private Instruction.* London, 1873.

NAC George Ripley and Charles A. Dana, eds., *New American Cyclopaedia.* New York, 1866–1867.

Introduction

1. His autobiography, *Fukuō jiden,* while brilliant, was written almost forty years later.

2. *FZS* 7: 250.

3. Sakuma's solution was to combine "Eastern ethics and Western technics" *(tōyō dōtoku, seiyō geijutsu).* Others spoke of "the trunk and the branch," or used the slogan "Japanese soul and Western learning" *(wakon yōsai),* a reformulation of the earlier "Japanese soul and Chinese learning" *(wakon kansai).*

4. R. H. van Gulik, "Kakkaron, a Japanese Echo of the Opium War," *Monumenta Serica* 4 (1939–1940): 539.

5. R. H. Blyth, *Japanese Humour* (Tokyo, 1957), 13.

6. Muragaki Awaji-no-kami, *Kokai Nikki, the Diary of the First Japanese Embassy to the United States of America* (Tokyo, 1958), 42, 91, 104; *Mannen gannen daiichi kenbei shisetsu nikki* (Tokyo, 1977), 63, 128–129, 146–147. For a much more

critical interpretation of Muragaki's mindset, see Miyoshi Masao, *As We Saw Them* (Berkeley, 1979).

7. For the information on Fukuzawa's life, I have drawn on many sources; see the Bibliography.

8. In the Japanese original, the first volume of *Conditions in the West* is the *shohen* (or volume 1); the second is the *gaihen* (or supplementary volume); the third is the *nihen* (or volume 2). To avoid confusion, I refer to the third volume as the "third volume" and not as "volume 2."

1. Scottish Enlightenment and Stages of Civilization

1. Some scholars feel that the historical argument is primary and the metaphysical argument unimportant. It may be secondary but it is not unimportant. In his *Letter Concerning Toleration*, Locke wrote in 1689: "Those are not at all to be tolerated who deny the being of God. Promises, covenants and oaths, which are the bonds of human societies, can have no hold on an atheist." See Locke, *Two Treatises of Government and a Letter Concerning Toleration*, 148.

2. In writing this I have used Locke, *Two Treatises of Government*, ed. Peter Laslett (Cambridge, Eng., 1963).

3. Viewed from a distance, the Enlightenment seems to possess a unity of thought. But up close, it displays a bewildering variety, much of which has been analyzed in meticulous detail by scholars. In this work I make no attempt to view it as a whole. For an analysis of the French, as well as the Scottish, aspects of the stages of civilization, I recommend a book to which I am much indebted: Ronald L. Meek, *Social Science and the Ignoble Savage* (Cambridge, Eng., 1976).

4. Adam Smith, *Lectures on Jurisprudence* (Oxford, 1978), 107. Smith began lectures at Glasgow in 1851. The student notes on which this account is based were taken in 1762–1763 and 1766.

5. "The History of America," in William Robertson, *The Works of William Robertson* (London, 1827), 6: 269. Robertson was the principal of Edinburgh University during its years of greatness between 1762 and 1793. When the University of London was founded in 1836, it was modeled not on Oxford or Cambridge, but on Edinburgh.

6. Ibid., 5: 273.

7. Turgot observed the same phenomenon in the cities of northern France. See Turgot, *Turgot on Progress, Sociology, and Economics*. Scholars debate the question of who was the first to enunciate a theory of stages, Turgot or Smith.

8. Adam Smith, *Lectures on Justice, Police Revenue, and Arms* (Oxford, 1896), 107–108.

9. Smith, *Jurisprudence*, 15–16.

10. Smith, *Justice*, 15.

11. Ibid., 14–15.

12. Smith, *Jurisprudence*, 404.

13. Ibid., 16.

14. Ibid.

15. Ibid.

16. Adam Ferguson, *An Essay on the History of Civil Society* (Edinburgh, 1966).

17. Ferguson was not alone in his negative view of Rousseau. Robertson's

comment was typical of the Scots: "Other philosophers have supposed that man arrives at his highest dignity and excellence long before he reaches the stage of refinement; and, in the rude simplicity of savage life, displays an elevation of sentiment, an independence of mind, and a warmth of attachment, for which it is vain to search among the members of polished societies. They seem to consider that as the most perfect state which is the least civilized. They describe the manners of rude Americans with such rapture, as if they proposed them for models to the rest of the species. These contradictory theories have been proposed with equal confidence, and uncommon powers of genius and eloquence have been exerted, in order to clothe them with an appearance of truth." Robertson, *Works*, 6:274. A more recent and sympathetic view of Rousseau is Robert N. Bellah's "Rousseau on Society and the Individual" in *Jean-Jacques Rousseau, the Social Contract and the First and Second Discourses (Rethinking the Western Tradition series)*, ed. Susan Dunn (New Haven, 2002).

18. Ferguson, *Essay on the History of Civil Society*, 8.

19. Ibid., 6–7.

20. Ibid., 1.

21. Ibid., 261.

22. Ibid., 242.

23. Ibid., 208.

24. Ibid., 206–207.

25. Ibid., 191.

26. Ibid., xiii–xli.

27. David Hume, *Of the Standard of Taste and other Essays* (New York, 1950), 50.

28. John Millar, *Observations Concerning the Distinction of Ranks in Society* (London, 1771), xiii, xiv.

29. Robertson, *Works*, 5: 383–384.

30. Ibid., 5: 255.

31. Smith, *Jurisprudence*, 15.

32. Ferguson, *Essay on the History of Civil Society*, 81.

33. John Millar, *Origin of the Distinction of Ranks* (London, 1781), 3.

34. Smith, *Jurisprudence*, 221.

35. Anand Chitnis, *The Scottish Enlightenment* (London, 1976), 94.

36. Millar, *Origin*, 3, 5.

37. Chitnis, *Scottish Enlightenment*, 117.

38. Ibid.

39. Millar, *Observations*, v–vi.

40. Voltaire (1694–1778) and Montesquieu (1680–1755) were possible exceptions. But even Voltaire, while reaching out to the rest of the world, molded it to fit his European purposes. And Montesquieu's *Lettres persanes* were more Montesquieu than *persanes*.

41. In his generation, Hamilton was the principal representative of the Scottish "intuitional school," a term that refers to the so-called commonsense philosophy of Reid and Stewart. To oversimplify, this philosophy posits first that the images of perception are of a real world, and second, that humans possess a "moral faculty." Hamilton used Kant to defend Reid against John Stuart Mill, who, in 1865, wrote a critique titled *An Examination of Sir William Hamilton's Philosophy*.

42. Joseph Blau has suggested that the Civil War led Wayland to strengthen

his criticism of slavery and to tone down his moral critique of war in the 1865 edition; otherwise the new edition was the same as the old. Wayland died the year that the new edition was published. See Joseph L. Blau, ed., *Francis Wayland: The Elements of Moral Science* (Cambridge, 1963), xlvi–xli.

2. American Geography Textbooks

Epigraph: From a lecture at Moscow University, quoted in Ronald Meek, *Social Science and the Ignoble Savage* (Cambridge, Eng., 1976), 5. Denitsky studied ethics and jurisprudence with Adam Smith and civil law with John Millar at Glasgow University between 1761 and 1767.

1. Jedidiah Morse, *Elements of Geography* (Boston, 1801), 39.
2. Ibid., 54.
3. Ibid., 66. A few years later, Richard Phillips wrote in the same vein: "Europe is the smallest of the grand divisions . . . of the world, but it is inhabited by the most active and intelligent race of people." "Africa, now reduced to a state of general barbarism, once contained several kingdoms and states, eminent for arts and commerce." Richard Phillips, *An Easy Grammar of Geography* (Boston, 1807), 21, 48. (This work is sometimes listed as *J. Goldsmith's Geography*.)
4. H. G. Stafford, *General Geography and Rudiments of Useful Knowledge* (Hudson, NY, 1809), 152, 35. A. F. Tytler (also listed in catalogs under Lord Woodhouselee), in his *Elements of General History, Ancient and Modern* (1809), 12–13, wrote, "The progress from barbarism to civilization is slow." Nathaniel Wright in *A Geographical Vocabulary* (Portland, ME, 1813), 38–39, contrasted Pacific islanders, who are "savages, some mild in their manners, others ferocious and bloody," and peoples in the interior of Asia, who are "generally barbarians," with the inhabitants of Europe, who are "refined in their manners and generally governed by wholesome laws." Daniel Adams (1773–1864), in *Geography; or, A Description of the World in Three Parts* (Boston, 1818), 92, 204, wrote of America prior to Columbus as "a vast . . . wilderness, but sparingly inhabited by a people mostly rude and savage." He mentioned Mexico and Peru, where "the Indians had made some progress in civilization and the arts." In contrast, in Europe progress in the arts and sciences had been "carried to the greatest perfection."
5. Joseph E. Worcester, *Elements of Geography, Ancient and Modern* (Boston, 1819), 18.
6. It might be noted that earlier writers often used "enlightened" as a descriptive term to indicate a high level of development, though not as the name of a stage. For example, in *The Material Creation: Being a Compendious System of Universal Geography and Popular Astronomy* (Dedham, MA, 1818), 5, Hermann Mann described the racial makeup of the peoples of the world and commented: "Europeans, and their descendants in America," now constitute "the most noble and enlightened part of the great family of mankind."
7. Ibid., 48–49.
8. William C. Woodbridge, *Rudiments of Geography* (Hartford, CT, 1821), 47–49, and *A System of Universal Geography, Ancient and Modern* (Hartford, CT, 1824), 166–167. The inclusion of an "enlightened stage" was imitated by some but not by all. Worcester, in a publication of 1827, continued to use "civilized" as his

highest stage. Conrad Malte-Brun (1775–1826), a Danish geographer living in Paris and writing in French, in 1812 published *Précis de la Géographie*. Under the heading "classes des nations," he distinguished between "sauvages," "barbares ou demi-civilisés," and "civilisés." An English version of the Malte-Brun geography, titled *Universal Geography*, was published in Boston in 1824, with a discussion of the stages on pp. 599–600. Samuel Griswold Goodrich (1793–1860), a prolific writer of textbooks, translated Malte-Brun, or had him translated, and published *A System of School Geography, Chiefly Derived from Malte-Brun* in 1830. Like the original, it discerned only three stages. Years later, Goodrich felt a need to make further distinctions among civilized societies (or felt it necessary to compete with other texts that did so), and wrote of societies that were "civilized" and of others that were "more civilized." Still other writers included an "enlightened" stage, but disagreed on the number of preceding stages. Jesse Olney (1798–1872) in 1830 listed four, as did Nathaniel G. Huntington (1785–1838) in 1834, while Roswell C. Smith (1797–1875) in 1835 listed five. See Olney, *A Practical System of Modern Geography* (Hartford, CT, 1830), 253–254; Huntington, *A System of Modern Geography* (Hartford, CT, 1834), 16–17; Smith, *Smith's Geography: Geography on the Productive System* (Philadelphia, 1835), 83.

9. My brief sketch of textbooks is admittedly incomplete. Had they been available, I would have surveyed British and French geographies. It is possible that some future scholar will discover that French works, such as those of Malte-Brun, were more influential than I have indicated. Future scholars may also map the intervening layers of high-level geographical literature that certainly exist between the Scottish philosophical works and the American geographies.

10. See Albert Craig, "Fukuzawa Yukichi and Shinmon Berihente," *Kindai Nihon kenkyū* 19 (2002).

11. Hayashiya Tatsusaburō, *Bunmei kaika no kenkyū* (Tokyo, 1979), 7. The name of the year-period was probably taken from the *Book of Changes*, one of the Chinese classics.

12. *FZS* 1: 346, 349; *Lippincott's Pronouncing Gazetteer* (Philadelphia, 1866), 1288. In speaking of the Romans in the section on English history, Fukuzawa uses *"bunmei no michi o hiraki"* for "introduced . . . their . . . civilization," and *"kaika ni omomuki"* to describe the reestablishment of Christianity during the 600s. See *FZS* 1: 353, 354.

13. *FZS* 17: 31, 35. The date 1866/11/07 refers to the seventh day of the eleventh month of the second year of the Keiō year-period (which mostly coincides with 1866). That is, it follows the Japanese solar-lunar calendar in use at the time. (Japan switched to the Western calendar on 1872/12/03, which became January 1, 1873.)

14. *Dictionary of American Biography* (New York: 1928), 13: 61.

15. Two titles appear on the title page of the book. The first is *Mitchell's School Geography*, followed by the number of the edition. Beneath this is a second title: *A System of Modern Geography, Comprising a Description of the Present State of the World, and Its Five Great Divisions, America, Europe, Asia, Africa, and Oceania, with Their Several Empires, Kingdoms, States, Territories, etc.* In the National Union Catalog, the book is sometimes listed under the one title and sometimes under the other. The book was published in Philadelphia, with earlier editions by Cowperthwait, Desilver, & Butler, and later editions by E. H. Butler & Co.

16. The full title is *Cornell's High School Geography: Forming Part Third of a Systematic Series of School Geographies, Comprising a Description of the World* (New York, 1866).

17. These pictures also appear in *Cornell's Primary School Geography*.

18. Mitchell, *Mitchell's School Geography*, 77; *FZS* 1: 396–397. Following this passage, Mitchell wrote: "The creation of the world, according to the book of Genesis, took place nearly 6,000 years ago; so that, supposing the average duration of life to have been always the same, about 180 generations of men would have existed since that time." Fukuzawa omitted this as he did all explicit references to the Bible.

19. Cornell, *Cornell's High School Geography*, 13.

20. Mitchell, *Mitchell's School Geography*, 44.

21. The use of "enlightened" in various early nineteenth-century geographies and in the specific geographies used by Fukuzawa is noteworthy in that some scholars, while allowing that *bunmei* was a translation-term for "civilization," have persisted in maintaining that *kaika* was not a translation-term but was independently arrived at by Fukuzawa. They base their argument on the asseration by the *Oxford English Dictionary* that "Enlightenment," as a descriptive term for eighteenth-century thought, came into use only in 1865. That is to say, it appeared after Fukuzawa established the term *kaika*. It is now crystal clear, however, that the dating of "Enlightenment" is not the issue. Fukuzawa was not translating "Enlightenment" but "enlightened," an adjective that had been used for decades as the name of a stage.

22. *FZS* 2: 463–465.

23. The last printing of the older *Mitchell* was in 1866, and the first printing of the new *Mitchell* was in 1865; there was an overlap of a year. Both were published by E. H. Butler & Co. of Philadelphia. The full title of the revised work is *Mitchell's New School Geography*. This is followed, beneath a line, by a second title: *A System of Modern Geography, Physical, Political, and Descriptive*. In the *National Union Catalog*, this edition, too, is sometimes listed under the first title and sometimes under the second. At the beginning of *Handbook*, Fukuzawa briefly lists the English works he used. Among them was the 1866 new edition of Mitchell's geography. See *FZS* 2: 456.

24. Mitchell, *Mitchell's New School Geography*, 35–38; *FZS* 2: 463–464.

25. Why *kaika bunmei* and not *bunmei kaika*? I suspect it was a printer's error, but it may be that Fukuzawa was still experimenting. After this publication, he used only *bunmei kaika*. Other writers who followed in Fukuzawa's footsteps were even looser in their usage; Nishi Amane often used *kaika* as a translation for civilization.

26. *FZS* 2: 463.

27. In *FZS* 2: 456, in his introduction to *Handbook*, Fukuzawa lists his Western texts. One listing is Cornell, *Cornell's High School Geography*, with a 1867 publication date. Since he had already used *Cornell's High School Geography* in his 1866 *Conditions I*, this must have been a later printing. He probably bought it at Appleton's in New York in 1867. It differs only in details from the old. Since he used it for *Handbook*, he no doubt used it for *All the Countries* as well.

28. For example, the original passage describing savages as having "no system of laws or morals" is translated in *Handbook* as "*hōritsu o shirazu, katsute reigi no*

nanimonotaru o shirazu," but in *All the Countries of the World,* it is rendered as *"hōritsu o shirazu, reigi no michi naku."* The statement that barbarous nomads "raise various kinds of grain for food" is translated in the *Handbook* as *"kōsaku no hō o shirite, shokubutsu no shurui ōshi,"* whereas in *All the Countries of the World,* it becomes *"yaya nōgyō no michi o kokoroete, gokoku* [the five grains] *o kuu mono mo ari."*

29. *FZS* 2: 463–465, 663–665.

30. Ibid. 2: 611–612.

31. Mitchell, *Mitchell's New School Geography,* 42.

32. *Rainichi seiyō jinmei jiten* (Tokyo, 1983), 205; *Nihon gaikōshi jiten* (Tokyo, 1992), 448–449.

33. *FZS* 21: 357–359.

34. Ibid. 21: 357–360.

3. John Hill Burton's *Political Economy*

1. *PE* 6.

2. Fukuzawa had Burton's *Political Economy* in his possession by 1866 or possibly earlier. He may have bought it in London in 1862, but, more likely, he found it in the Gaikokugata library. We know he had it in 1866 since he translated a few lines from it on the opening page of *Conditions I.* I would conjecture, however, that he read the entire work and grasped its import after the publication of *Conditions I.*

3. *FZS* 1: 385.

4. John Hill Burton, *The Book Hunter* (Edinburgh, 1882), xlii. This edition has a memoir on Burton.

5. Burton's *Political Economy,* originally published in London and Edinburgh in 1852, was then reprinted a number of times. The last printing I have examined, that of 1873, is no different from the first. See Albert Craig, "John Hill Burton and Fukuzawa Yukichi," in *Kindai Nihon kenkyū* 1 (1984). In 1852, Burton also wrote, for the same educational course, a do-it-yourself manual on emigration, a topic of interest in Scotland at the time.

6. *PE* 49.

7. *PE,* the unnumbered page following the title page.

8. My understanding of this first great shift toward a more secular worldview owes much to the insightful writings of Watanabe Hiroshi. See, for example, his *Kinsei Nihon shakai to Sōgaku* (Tokyo, 1985). Confucian teachings had entered Japan centuries earlier but they reached a critical mass only during the Tokugawa era. There were, of course, more than two schools of Confucianism.

9. Fukuzawa's son later wrote that among the Chinese schools his father favored that of Zhu Xi but was also a great admirer of Ogyū Sorai. See Fukuzawa Sanpachi, *Chichi Yukichi o kataru* (Tokyo, 1958), 6.

10. *PE* 1; *FZS* 1: 389.

11. Ibid. Fukuzawa felt that the goal of "enjoyment" was insufficiently lofty. He wrote instead, "If humans do not work, they will achieve nothing."

12. Though Fukuzawa often used *zōbutsushu,* in the passage quoted earlier he did not. He did, however, translate "ACTIVE BEING" as "created being" or *zōbutsu,* which implied the work of a *zōbutsushu.*

13. Morohashi's authoritative *Dai Kanwa jiten* has *zōbutsusha* (*sha* means per-

son) but not *zōbutsushu* (*shu* means master). Fukuzawa was not the first to use the term. I noted its appearance in Mitsukuri Shōgo, *Kon'yo zushiki-ho* (1845) 7a (each numbered page has two sides).

14. *PE* 2; *FZS* 1: 390.

15. *PE* 2–3; *FZS* 1: 390–391. In 1870, Fukuzawa reiterated Burton's views on marriage and women's rights in *A Farewell to Nakatsu*. See *FZS* 20: 50. I cite the passage in my concluding chapter.

16. *PE* 2; *FZS* 1: 390–391.

17. *PE* 3; *FZS* 1: 391. In this passage, and in the quoted passages that follow, the English text is from Burton and the Japanese terms in parentheses are from Fukuzawa's translation. Fukuzawa appears to have adopted Burton's view of society. In *An Encouragement of Learning* he used the same language and wrote, "Humans are social by nature *(gunkyo o konomi)* and cannot exist alone and isolated *(doppo koritsu o ezu)*." Or again, "Man's original nature is to enjoy socializing with others *(ganrai hito no sei wa majiwari o konomu)*, and only by circumstances will he come to dislike it." In *Outline of Theories of Civilization*, too, he wrote: "From the beginning, humans are by nature social. Alone and isolated, their abilities and intelligence cannot develop." *FZS* 3: 87, 114; *FZS* 4: 38.

18. Since Fukuzawa did not accept, and possibly did not understand, Locke's idea of a "state of nature," it follows that he did not accept the social contract in Locke's sense of the term. But he did feel that members of civilized societies ought to obey the (civil) law. If they did not, as Burton put it, they would be "stealing from society one of its benefits." If this moral dictum is equated with the social contract, then we might say that Fukuzawa accepted a watered-down version of the contract. Blackstone, translated by Fukuzawa in the third volume of *Outline*, accepted the ideas of Locke. Wayland, whose ideas influenced *An Encouragement of Learning*, was closer to Burton.

19. *PE* 10; *FZS* 1: 399.

20. *PE* 11–12; *FZS* 1: 401. In this instance, I have retranslated Fukuzawa's Japanese back into English to show how he handled the passage.

21. *PE* 10–11; *FZS* 1: 400.

22. In his 1868 translation of Burton, Fukuzawa used a milder combination of terms, "to emulate and vie" *(aihagemi aikisou koto)* to render the chapter title, but in the text, he used the stronger verb *arasou* in the phrase *"saki o arasowazaru mono nashi."* *PE* 399; *FZS* 7: 148–149.

23. *PE* 6–7; *FZS* 1: 395.

24. *PE* 6; *FZS* 1: 395.

25. *PE* 7; *FZS* 1: 396.

26. *FZS* 1: 392–394.

27. *PE* 10–11; *FZS* 1: 400. In writing of "Oriental nations," Burton meant the nations of the Middle East, but Fukuzawa rendered this as "East Asian nations" *(tōyō shokoku)*.

28. *PE* 36.

29. *PE* 19–20; *FZS* 1: 413–414.

30. *PE* 20; *FZS* 1: 414.

31. *PE* 18; *FZS* 1: 412.

32. *PE* 22; *FZS* 1: 416. In the paragraph preceding the poem, Fukuzawa re-

placed "vagrants" with the familiar Japanese image of "beggars living under a bridge."

33. *PE* 15; *FZS* 1: 408.

34. *PE* 21; *FZS* 1: 415. Fukuzawa rarely injected his own feelings into his translation-text, but on reading of the German feudal lord, he added, "Such cruelty is beyond description!"

35. *PE* 23; *FZS* 1: 417.

36. *PE* 16–17; *FZS* 1: 410.

37. *PE* 26; *FZS* 1: 420–421.

38. *PE* 24. Fukuzawa deleted this passage from his translation in the supplementary volume because he had already presented it in *Conditions I*. *FZS* 1: 289.

39. *PE* 25. Fukuzawa used this passage from *Political Economy* three times to make clear the distinction between the form and reality (*mei* and *jitsu*) of a government: once in *Conditions I* (*FZS* 1: 289) in his discussion of the three forms of government, monarchy, aristocracy, and democracy; a second time in the supplementary volume of *Conditions* (*FZS* 1: 419), and a third time in *Outline of Theories of Civilization* (*FZS* 4: 43).

40. *PE* 25.

41. *PE* 28; *FZS* 1: 423.

42. *PE* 26; *FZS* 1: 420–421.

43. *PE* 12–14. In his *Political and Social Economy* written three years earlier, Burton wrote an even more vitriolic attack on "artificial systems." "We approach the doctrines of the Socialists and the Communists in that spirit of pure hostility in which those who are free to declare their own opinions . . . discuss whatever they consider to be fraught with evil."

44. *PE* 14.

45. *PE* 27; *FZS* 1: 421.

46. *PE* 29–32; *FZS* 1: 424–427. Two pages later, Burton wrote again of misplaced trust in "theoretical novelties." Fukuzawa rendered this as *"midara ni shinki o konomi, shijō no kūron o shinjite."* *FZS* 1: 427. Fukuzawa also spoke of the benefits of slow, peaceful change over the centuries in *Outline of Theories of Civilization. FZS* 4: 29.

47. Burton did concede that oppressive conditions at the end of the eighteenth century had led to the French Revolution.

48. *PE* 31; *FZS* 1: 427.

49. *PE* 53; *FZS* 1: 461–462.

50. *PE* 37; *FZS* 1: 435–436. To inform his readers how to interpret this event, Fukuzawa described it as a "colorful story showing an extreme example of stupidity."

51. Ibid.

52. *PE* 52; *FZS* 1: 460–461. I have grouped together in this section passages that in *Burton* were distributed through his text.

53. *PE* 53–54; *FZS* 1: 463.

54. *FZS* 19: 368, *Keiō Gijuku no ki*. Should *tenshin* be translated as "nature's truth" or as "heaven's truth"? Both are possibilities. If we translate it as "nature," we must remember that for Fukuzawa, "nature" included morality (*jindō*). It was more than "nature" in the modern sense of the term. But if we translate it as

"heaven's truth," we should be careful not to read too much into "heaven." Fuku-zawa's school was given the name "Keiō" when it moved to its new Mita location in the fourth month of 1868, before the fourth year of the Keiō year-period had changed to the first year of the Meiji year-period.

4. Invention, the Engine of Progress

Epigraph: NAC 16: 291; *FZS* 1: 404. Fukuzawa bought the *Cyclopaedia* in New York in 1867. Francis Jeffrey was a literary critic, Scottish judge, lord rector of Glasgow University in 1820 and 1822, and founder and editor of the *Edinburgh Review*.

1. The chapters of the report covering the mission's stay in England have been edited and annotated by Matsuzawa Hiroaki as "Eikoku tansaku." See *Seiyō kenbunshū* (in the series *Nihon shisō taikei*) (Tokyo, 1974). In the same volume, also see Matsuzawa's insightful "Kaidai."

2. *FZS* 19: 202–204.

3. *FZS* 4: 133.

4. *FZS* 1: 28–29. In his essay "Kaikoku," Maruyama Masao writes of the Rakuzenkai, a nongovernmental organization formed by Nakamura Masanao and others to establish a school for the blind. *Maruyama Masao-shū*, vol. 8 (Tokyo, 1996), 81–82.

5. *FZS* 1: 313.

6. *FZS* 1: 315.

7. *FZS* 1: 316–317.

8. *FZS* 1: 316.

9. Alexander Fraser Tytler (Lord Woodhouselee), *Elements of General History, Ancient and Modern* (Concord, NH, 1831). A professor at the University of Edin-burgh, Tytler was born in 1747 and died in 1813. Before and after his death, his book went through a substantial number of British and American editions. The Gaikokugata library, now at the Aoi Bunko, apparently had an 1861 edition, pub-lished by Henry Bohn in London. Fukuzawa may have used it. An 1853 Bohn edi-tion contains the same material I cite in this chapter. I have used an 1831 edition published in Concord, New Hampshire. In these chapters, it differs little from the Bohn edition. For cited passages, see 160–162, 227–230, and 419–420. Different editions vary slightly in their pagination.

10. Ibid., 160. In Japan today the word *bungaku* means "literature." But in Fukuzawa's translations, it usually means "learning." In this instance, even though Tytler's original title-word is "literature," I suspect, judging from his choice of con-tent, that Fukuzawa still meant "learning."

11. *FZS* 1: 301. After listing the fields, Fukuzawa added an explanatory note in small print: "Western scholarship has as its goal the investigation of the principles *(ri)* of the 10,000 things, clarifying their functions *(yō)*, and benefiting mankind by having people fully develop their heaven-given (or natural) mental faculties."

12. Tytler, *Elements*, 239; *FZS* 1: 301–302.

13. Tytler, *Elements*, 447; *FZS* 1: 302.

14. Every now and then Fukuzawa inserts into his translations bits of informa-tion not given in his primary English text. The 1423 date (Tytler says 1440) for the invention of printing is one such bit. Of books used by Fukuzawa, the only one, in-

sofar as I could ascertain, that is even close (1424) is W. T. Brande and G. W. Cox, *A Dictionary of Science, Literature, and Art* (London, 1865–1867), 3: 64.

15. Tytler, *Elements,* 447; *FZS* 1: 302. I have cited the original list.

16. *PE,* 11; *FZS* 1: 400–401.

17. *FZS* 1: 402–404; *NAC* 16: 288–293. These pages cover the materials on the Watt quotations that follow.

18. *NAC* 15: 83–84.

19. *FZS* 1: 405.

20. *NAC* 15: 85; *FZS* 1: 407.

21. *PE* 54–55.

22. *PE* 57; *FZS* 1: 467–468. Fukuzawa's translation of this passage is straightforward. He translates "nice," which in this context probably means "requiring careful definition," as "even more beautiful" *(issō no bi o tsukushi)*.

23. Francis Wayland (1796–1865) was a scientifically minded Baptist divine, the president of Brown University, and an important influence on Fukuzawa. The first edition of his *Elements of Political Economy* was published in 1837, the last in 1886. The principal publisher was Gould and Lincoln of Boston. I use the 1860 edition.

24. Francis Wayland, *The Elements of Political Economy* (Boston, 1837), 53–54.

25. Ibid., 55–56.

26. Brande and Cox, *Dictionary of Science, Literature, and Art,* 2: 833–835.

27. *NAC* 13: 28.

28. *NAC* 13: 28–29.

29. *FZS* 19: 152. His *Keiō sannen nikki* tells us he visited the patent office on the twenty-eighth day of the fourth month (or May 31) in 1867.

30. *FZS* 1: 472.

31. W. T. Brande and G. W. Cox, *A Dictionary of Science, Literature, and Art* (London, 1866), 2: 833–834.

32. *NAC* 5: 703–704.

5. An Outline of Theories of Civilization

Epigraph: FZS 4: 72.

1. In Japanese, *ron* means discussion or theory. (A *giron* is an argument, a *tōron* a debate, and *shinkaron* is the theory of evolution.) But what did Fukuzawa have in mind when he titled his work an "Outline of a *Ron* on Civilization?" If this is translated as "Outline of a Discussion of Civilization," there is no problem. But if we use "theory" instead of "discussion," then we must choose between the singular and the plural—the Japanese *ron* can be either. Until now, the title has always been translated as "An Outline of a Theory of Civilization." I have used, instead, the plural. I have not made this change lightly. Reading the book together with the English sources, it seemed clear to me that Fukuzawa was presenting three separate theories. The theories, to be sure, have much in common, since they are all answers to the same question of why the West developed as it did. But, as will become clear, they are structurally different with different emphases and approaches. Burton and Mitchell had a socio-political-cultural model; Buckle stressed intelligence; and Guizot, balance. Fukuzawa was well aware of what they had in common. Based on

their common features, he might have joined them together into a single, master theory. But he chose instead to present them sequentially—with only a few bits and pieces appearing out of order. Fukuzawa's intent, I would judge, was to present theories, not a theory.

2. *FZS* 17: 152.

3. In his definition, Fukuzawa combined the "savage" and "barbarous" stages. Elsewhere, he occasionally used the term *sōmai* to describe the lower reaches of barbarism.

4. *FZS* 4: 17.

5. Ibid.

6. Ibid. It is notable that Fukuzawa used *bunmei* and not *bunmei kaika* as he had earlier. Had he realized that the composite term was not widely used in the West?

7. *FZS* 4: 16–17.

8. *FZS* 4: 107. For a full English translation of *Bunmeiron no gairyaku*, see David A. Dilworth and G. Cameron Hurst, *Fukuzawa Yukichi's "An Outline of a Theory of Civilization"* (Tokyo, 1973). For the sake of my argument, I have made more literal translations, but I always checked my translation against theirs and often borrowed phrases from their most useful work.

9. *FZS* 4: 18–19.

10. François Guizot, *General History of Civilization in Europe* (New York, 1867), 19; *FZS* 4: 38–39. This simile appears in the third chapter of *Outline*, not in chapters 8 and 9, where Fukuzawa discusses Guizot.

11. *FZS* 4: 20.

12. *FZS* 4: 18.

13. Guizot, *General History*, 18, 32; *FZS* 4: 4.

14. This 1876 essay became chapter 15 of *An Encouragement of Learning (Gakumon no susume)*. In terms of content, I think of it almost as an addendum to *Outline*. The chapters of *Encouragement* were written between 1872 and 1876. It is available in an English translation by David A. Dilworth and Umeyo Hirano titled *Fukuzawa Yukichi's "An Encouragement of Learning"* (Tokyo, 1969).

15. *FZS* 3: 124.

16. *FZS* 3: 126.

17. The title of the editorial, "Datsuaron," was provocative, but the content was close to what he had written in 1875. *FZS* 10: 238–240. Tanaka Akira, in *Nihon no ayunda michi*, 165–167, discusses the international context of the editorial, and cites an earlier 1883 publication, *Gaikōron*, which contains similar ideas.

18. *FZS* 3: 18.

19. *FZS* 3: 44.

20. *FZS* 4: 23–26. Fukuzawa's comparison makes no explicit mention of stages. But since he is talking about two countries that he had earlier listed as "half-civilized," he seems to be saying that there can be significant differences even between countries at the same stage.

21. *FZS* 4: 26–30.

22. *FZS* 4: 34–35, 116–119.

23. *FZS* 4: 35.

24. *FZS* 4: 35.

25. Both essays are in *FZS* 5.

26. Henry T. Buckle, *History of Civilization in England*, 2 vols. (New York, 1858). (Fukuzawa may have used a later printing.)

27. Ibid., 1: 15, 29.

28. Ibid., 1: 101.

29. Ibid., 1: 93–94, 109.

30. Ibid., 1: 17–24; *FZS* 4: 55–56, 60.

31. *FZS* 4: 66.

32. Buckle, *History of Civilization*, 1: 126.

33. *FZS* 4: 51.

34. Buckle, *History of Civilization*, 1: 129, 131.

35. *FZS* 4: 70.

36. *FZS* 4: 74. Fukuzawa returns to the tenuous ties between people and emperor later in *Outline: FZS* 4: 187–189.

37. *FZS* 4: 75.

38. *FZS* 4: 116.

39. *FZS* 4: 119–122.

40. I have used the 1867 C. S. Henry edition published by Appleton and Co. in New York. It is the ninth American edition based on the second English edition.

41. Guizot, *General History*, 35–39.

42. Ibid., 37.

43. Ibid., 40.

44. *FZS* 4: 145.

45. *FZS* 4: 145–152.

46. *FZS* 4: 146.

47. *FZS* 4: 153.

48. *FZS* 4: 153–154.

49. *FZS* 4: 152, 155–156.

50. *FZS* 4: 156–159.

51. *FZS* 4: 159, 163.

52. *FZS* 4: 163.

53. *FZS* 4: 160.

54. *FZS* 7: 244. In his autobiography, Fukuzawa claims that he never gave a thought to curing Japan's ills. True, he never thought of becoming a politician. But he certainly worked tirelessly as a publicist to point out Japan's failings and to persuade others to attend to them. See Matsuzawa Hiroaki's chapter "Fukuzawa Yukichi, a Diagnostician of Government" in his *Nihon seiji shisō* (Tokyo, 1993), 25–32.

55. *FZS* 6: 38–39.

56. *FZS* 6: 40–46.

57. *FZS* 6: 47–48. The entire essay is contained in *FZS* 6: 31–70.

58. *FZS* 4: 207–208.

59. *FZS* 17: 15–16.

60. *FZS* 17: 77.

61. *FZS* 20: 53. The passage is from "A Farewell to Nakatsu" *(Nakatsu ryūbetsu no sho)*, a long letter to friends in his former domain in which he explained why he would not live there. It has been translated by Kiyooka Eiichi in *Fukuzawa Yukichi on Education* (Tokyo, 1985), 35–42, and by David Oberman and Kayano Tomoatsu in *Hokkaido Law Review* 40, nos. 5–6 (1990).

62. *FZS* 3: 42.

63. *FZS* 3: 107.

64. *FZS* 17: 175–176.

65. Ibid.

66. *FZS* 4: 185.

67. *FZS* 4: 200.

68. *FZS* 4: 196–197. In a letter of April 29, 1875, to Tomita Tetsunosuke, Fukuzawa wrote: "Wanton acts by foreigners steadily increase. Recently, there have been two cases of rape. Who says that the white men of the Western nations represent civilization? They are truly inhuman white devils! Let Christianity eat shit! Rather than sending useless priests to our country to convert those who have no need of it, it would be far better if they appointed upright and humane *(ningenrashii)* men as ministers and consuls to punish those who rob and rape. When their citizens commit rape in a foreign land, the governments of British and American civilization not only fail to punish them, but their ministers and consuls take the side of the rapists and put pressure on our country. Unspeakable white devils!" Ibid. 17: 184.

69. *FZS* 7: 660. Fukuzawa's criticism of Western nations and their commercial practices did not prevent him from having considerable contacts with Westerners in Tokyo. He regularly invited American scholars to teach at Keiō. In 1883, he urged his son Ichitarō, who was "poor at socializing and apt to withdraw," "to learn from Americans and strive, morning and night, to get on *amiably* with others." "Eventually," he added, "what you have put into practice will become your nature. It is most important that you deepen the basis for lifetime *happiness*." Ibid. 17: 576.

70. *FZS* 4: 190–191.

71. *FZS* 4: 202.

72. *FZS* 4: 200–203.

73. *FZS* 4: 203.

74. *FZS* 4: 179–184, 205. On the first morning of each new year, retainers of the Itō House in Hyūga exchanged similar warnings, directed against their traditional enemies, the Shimazu of Satsuma. Fukuzawa cites this as a precedent.

75. *FZS* 20: 49–50.

76. Carmen Blacker, *The Japanese Enlightenment: A Study of the Writings of Fukuzawa Yukichi* (Cambridge, Eng., 1964), 150, 159. Blacker's most readable book is the pioneer Western study of Fukuzawa's thought in the 1870s.

77. *FZS* 4: 23. By the time he wrote *Outline*, Fukuzawa had pretty much given up using the term *zōbutsushu*. As far as I have noted, this is its sole occurrence in the work. In using it, Fukuzawa may have been paraphrasing the following sentence by Guizot: "European civilization has, if I may be allowed the expression, at last penetrated into the ways of eternal truth—into the scheme of Providence;—it moves in the ways which God has prescribed." Guizot, *General History*, 40.

78. *FZS* 4: 44–45.

79. *FZS* 4: 3.

80. *FZS* 4: 194–200.

81. *FZS* 4: 451–453.

82. *FZS* 5: 105–106.

83. *FZS* 5: 107–109.

Reflections

1. Donald Keene, *Modern Japanese Literature* (New York, 1956) 32.

2. There is a huge literature in Japanese on the civilization and enlightenment movement. It would make a splendid topic for a Ph.D. thesis. For further reading, the student might begin by reading Asukai Masamichi's *Bunmei kaika* for its penetrating interpretation, and Tanaka Akira's *Mikan no Meiji ishin*, 97–104, for its depiction of the popular response to the movement.

3. The best introduction to the Meirokusha is William R. Braisted's *Meiroku Zasshi, Journal of the Japanese Enlightenment* (Cambridge, 1976).

4. This passage may be found in ibid., 38. My translation is based on the text in *Meiji bunka zenshū* (Tokyo, 1928), 18.

5. Edward Morse, *Japan Day by Day* (Boston, 1917), 1: 284, 339–340.

6. Irokawa Daikichi, *The Culture of the Meiji Period*, trans. M. B. Jansen (Princeton, 1985), 108–113.

7. "Kaikoku" in *Maruyama Masao-shū* (Tokyo) 8 (1996): 81.

8. Itō Hirobumi, *Itōkō zenshū* (Tokyo, 1928), 2: 129–130, 145–146 (in the portion of the book labeled "Gakumon Enzetsu").

9. An ideology is usually something that someone else has. I try to use the term in a neutral sense: ideas that serve as the basis for a course of action. For a sophisticated analysis of ideology and a more comprehensive view of Meiji ideology, see Carol Gluck, *Japan's Modern Myths* (Princeton, 1985), chapter 1.

10. Alexander Gerschenkron, *Economic Backwardness in Historical Perspective* (Cambridge, 1962), 24. Henry Rosovsky has applied Gerschenkron's economic arguments to Japan in *Capital Formation in Japan* (Glencoe, IL, 1961).

11. Gerschenkron, *Economic Backwardness*, 25–26.

12. Erwin Baelz, *Awakening Japan: The Diary of a German Doctor* (Bloomington, IN, 1974), 16. Some scholars may object to calling the changes of the Meiji era a "revolution" because the changes were initiated from above, not from below. But in any revolution, the overthrow of the old regime always comes from somewhere "below," and the new leaders always implement changes from above. This renders the objection irrelevant. The same scholars may continue to protest, saying that in the Meiji Restoration the overthrow did not begin far enough below, and that the changes, however radical they may have been vis-à-vis Tokugawa institutions, were not "radical" enough to fit the European sense of the term "revolution." That may be. Nonetheless, the magnitude of change during the Meiji era still dwarfs that of many "proper revolutions." As for it being a "cultural revolution," the massive Meiji importation of Western culture was the first step on the road to the hybrid culture that Japanese enjoy today.

13. He made these observations in the context of introducing Buckle's statistical approach by which the mental laws of entire societies might be grasped. *FZS* 4: 53–54.

14. *FZS* 4: 53.

15. *FZS* 4: 53–54.

16. Sashi Tsutae, "Shippitsu memo mitsukaru," in *Mita hyōron* (August–September 1991). All of the information on the *Plan* is from this article.

17. Of all of the English sources that Fukuzawa used, Guizot makes the clear-

est argument for relativity. Did the statement in the *Plan* come from another source? Or had Fukuzawa read only Guizot's second chapter, which contains the argument?

18. Sashi Tsutae, "Shippitsu memo mitsukaru," 78.

19. Ibid., 77.

20. Ibid.

21. Ibid., 76.

22. See Raouf Abbas Hamed, *The Japanese and Egyptian Enlightenment* (published by the Institute for the Study of Languages and Cultures of Asia and Africa of Tokyo University of Foreign Studies in 1990 as *Studia Culturae Islamicae* 41), 144–145, 133; and Albert Hourani, *Arabic Thought in the Liberal Age, 1798–1939* (Oxford, 1962), chapter 4. Tahtawi's definition of the stages was clearly more "economic" than that of Fukuzawa. He may have included Egypt and the others on the grounds that they had agriculture and commerce. According to Hamed, Tahtawi mentions invention only in the most general terms, as one consequence of the advance of knowledge. Decades ago, I taught a seminar with Benjamin Schwartz and Nadav Safran in which students wrote essays comparing some aspect of China, Japan, and the Middle East. As one might expect, all of the papers concluded that, in comparison with the Middle East, Japan and China were much alike.

23. *FZS* 4: 4–5.

24. Are the elements in Guizot's analysis the same in all civilizations, or are there cultural differences? It might be easier to explain the "balance" in European civilization in terms of cultural differences in other areas of the world. But Guizot argues that "the very same variety of elements, the very same struggle" found in Europe "is also found elsewhere." See Guizot, *General History*, 40.

25. *FZS* 4: 3–4.

26. *FZS* 4: 4.

27. *FZS* 20: 50–51.

28. *FZS* 4: 5.

Bibliography

Adams, Daniel. *Geography; or, A Description of the World in Three Parts*. Boston, 1818.

Aida Kurakichi. *Fukuzawa Yukichi*. Tokyo, 1974.

Asai Kiyoshi. *Meiji ishin to gunken shisō*. Tokyo, 1968.

Asukai Masamichi. *Bunmei kaika*. Iwanami shinsho series. Tokyo, 1985.

Baelz, Erwin. *Awakening Japan: The Diary of a German Doctor*. Bloomington, IN, 1974.

Banno Junji. *Meiji demokurashi*. Tokyo, 2005.

Bellah, Robert N. "Rousseau on Society and the Individual." In Susan Dunn, ed., *Jean-Jacques Rousseau, the Social Contract and the First and Second Discourses (Rethinking the Western Tradition* series). New Haven, 2002.

Blacker, Carmen. *The Japanese Enlightenment: A Study of the Writings of Fukuzawa Yukichi*. Cambridge, 1964.

Blyth, R. H. *Japanese Humour*. Tokyo, 1957.

Braisted, William R. *"Meiroku Zasshi," Journal of the Japanese Enlightenment*. Cambridge, 1976.

Brande, W. T., and George W. Cox. *A Dictionary of Science, Literature, and Art*. Vols. 1–3. London, 1865.

Buckle, Henry T. *History of Civilization in England*. 2 vols. New York, 1858.

Chitnis, Anand. *The Scottish Enlightenment*. London, 1976.

Cornell, Sarah S. *Cornell's High School Geography: Forming Part Third of a Systematic Series of School Geographies, Comprising a Description of the World*. New York, 1866.

Craig, Albert. "Fukuzawa Yukichi and Shinmon Berihente." *Kindai Nihon kenkyū* (Tokyo) 19 (2002).

———. "Fukuzawa Yukichi no rekishi ishiki to bunmei kaika." *Mita Hyōron* (April 1985).

———. "Fukuzawa Yukichi, the Philosophical Foundations of Meiji Nationalism." In Robert Ward, ed., *Political Development in Modern Japan*. Princeton, 1968.

————. "John Hill Burton and Fukuzawa Yukichi." *Kindai Nihon kenkyū* (Tokyo) 1 (1984).

————. "Warupuranku on the Death of a Schoolmaster." *Kindai Nihon kenkyū* (Tokyo) 13 (1996).

deBary, W. Theodore, Carol Gluck, and Arthur E. Tiedemann, eds. *Sources of the Japanese Tradition*. 2d ed., vol. 2. New York, 2005.

Dictionary of American Biography. New York, 1928.

Dilworth, David A., and Umeyo Hirano, trans. *Fukuzawa Yukichi's "An Encouragement of Learning."* Tokyo, 1969.

Dilworth, David A., and G. Cameron Hurst, trans. *Fukuzawa Yukichi's "An Outline of a Theory of Civilization."* Tokyo, 1973.

Duke, Benjamin C., ed. *Ten Educators of Modern Japan: A Japanese Perspective*. Tokyo, 1989.

Ferguson, Adam. *An Essay on the History of Civil Society*. Edinburgh, 1966.

The First Japanese Embassy to the United States of America. Tokyo, 1920.

Fukuzawa Daishirō. *Chichi Fukuzawa Yukichi*. Tokyo, 1959.

Fukuzawa Sanpachi. *Chichi Yukichi o kataru*. Tokyo, 1958.

Fukuzawa Yukichi. *The Autobiography of Fukuzawa Yukichi*, trans. Kiyooka Eiichi. New York, 2007.

Fukuzawa Yukichi chosakushū. Tokyo, 2001–2003.

Fukuzawa Yukichi shokanshū. Tokyo, 2001.

Fukuzawa Yukichi zenshū. Tokyo, 1969–1971 (originally published in 1958). This is the critical source for all Fukuzawa studies. It was edited by Tomita Masafumi and Tsuchihashi Shun'ichi. The three volumes of *Seiyō jijō* are in vol. 1, *Shōchū bankoku ichiran* and *Sekai kunizukushi* are in vol. 2, *Gakumon no susume* is in vol. 3, and *Bunmeiron no gairyaku* is in vol. 4.

Gerschenkron, Alexander. *Economic Backwardness in Historical Perspective*. Cambridge, 1962.

Gluck, Carol. *Japan's Modern Myths*. Princeton, 1985.

Goodrich, Samuel G. *A System of School Geography, Chiefly Derived from Malte-Brun*. N.p., 1830.

Guizot, François. *General History of Civilization in Europe*. New York, 1867.

Hamed, Raouf Abbas, *The Japanese and Egyptian Enlightenment*. Tokyo, 1990.

Hayashiya Tatsusaburō. *Bunmei kaika no kenkyū*. Tokyo, 1979.

Hirayama Yō. *Fukuzawa Yukichi no shinjitsu*. Tokyo, 2004.

Hirota Masaki. *Fukuzawa Yukichi*. Tokyo, 1976.

————. *Fukuzawa Yukichi kenkyū*. Tokyo, 1976.

Hourani, Albert. *Arabic Thought in the Liberal Age, 1798–1939*. Oxford, Eng., 1962.

Hume, David. *Of the Standard of Taste and Other Essays*. New York, 1950.

Huntington, Nathaniel G. *A System of Modern Geography*. Hartford, CT, 1834.

Iida Kanae. *Fukuzawa Yukichi Kokumin kokkaron no sōshisha*. Tokyo, 1984.

Imanaga Seiji. *Fukuzawa Yukichi no shisō keisei*. Tokyo, 1979.

Inoue Isao. *Bunmei kaika*. Tokyo, 1986.

Irokawa Daikichi. *The Culture of the Meiji Period*. Trans. M. B. Jansen. Princeton, 1985.

Ishida Takeshi. *Kindai Nihon seiji bunka to gengo shōchō*. Tokyo, 1983.

————. *Nihon kindai shisōshi ni okeru hō to seiji*. Tokyo, 1976.

Itō Hirobumi. *Itōkō zenshū*, 3 vols. Tokyo, 1928.

Itō Masao. *Fukuzawa Yukichi ronkō*. Tokyo, 1969.

———. *Meijijin no mita Fukuzawa Yukichi*. Tokyo, 1970.

Jansen, Marius, and Gilbert Rozman, eds. *Japan in Transition from Tokugawa to Meiji*. Princeton, 1986.

Keene, Donald. *Anthology of Japanese Literature*. New York, 1955–1956.

Kinmouth, Earl H. *The Self-Made Man in Meiji Japanese Thought*. Berkeley, 1981.

Kiyooka, Eiichi. *Fukuzawa Yukichi on Education*. Tokyo, 1985.

Lippincott's Pronouncing Gazetteer: A Complete Pronouncing Gazetteer or Geographical Dictionary of the World. Philadelphia, 1866.

Locke, John. *Two Treatises of Government*. Ed. Peter Laslett. Cambridge, Eng., 1963.

———. *Two Treatises of Government and a Letter Concerning Toleration*. Ed. Ian Shapiro. New Haven, 2003.

Malte-Brun, Conrad. *Précis de la Géographie*. Paris, 1812.

———. *Universal Geography*. Boston, 1924.

Mann, Herman. *The Material Creation: Being a Compendious System of Universal Geography and Popular Astronomy*. Dedham, MA, 1818.

Mannen gannen daiichi kenbei shisetsu nikki. Tokyo, 1977.

Maruyama Masao. *Bunmeiron no gairyaku o yomu*. Iwanami shinsho series. Tokyo, 1986.

———. "Fukuzawa, Okakura, Uchimura" and "Fukuzawa Yukichi ni tsuite." In vol. 7 of *Maruyama Masao-shū*. Tokyo, 1995.

———. "Fukuzawa Yukichi" and "Fukuzawa Yukichi senshū dai-4 kan kaidai." In vol. 5 of *Maruyama Masao-shū*. Tokyo, 1995.

———. *Studies in the Intellectual History of Tokugawa Japan*. Tokyo, 1974.

Matsuzawa Hiroaki. "Eikoku tansaku." *Seiyō kenbunshū*. Nihon shisō taikei series. Tokyo, 1974.

———. "'Kaisetsu' in Fukuzawa Yukichi." *Bunmeiron no gairyaku*. Iwanami bunko series. Tokyo, 1995.

———. *Kindai Nihon no keisei to seiyō keiken*. Tokyo, 1993.

———. *Nihon seiji shisō*. Tokyo, 1993.

Meek, Ronald. *Social Science and the Ignoble Savage*. Cambridge, Eng., 1976.

Millar, John. *Observations Concerning the Distinction of Ranks in Society*. London, 1771.

———. *The Origin of the Distinction of Ranks*. London, 1781.

Mitchell, Samuel S. *Mitchell's New School Geography: A System of Modern Geography, Physical, Political, and Descriptive*. Philadelphia, 1866.

———. *Mitchell's School Geography: A System of Modern Geography, Comprising a Description of the Present State of the World, and Its Five Great Divisions, America, Europe, Asia, Africa, and Oceania, with Their Several Empires, Kingdoms, States, Territories, etc.* Philadelphia, 1866.

Mitsukuri Shōgo. *Kon'yo zushiki-ho*. Edo, 1845.

Miyamoto Moritarō. *Kindai Nihon seiji shisō no zahyō*. Tokyo, 1987.

Miyoshi Masao. *As We Saw Them*. Berkeley, 1979.

Morse, Edward. *Japan Day by Day*. Boston, 1917.

Morse, Jedidiah. *Elements of Geography*. Boston, 1801.

Muragaki Awaji-no-kami. *The Diary of the First Japanese Embassy to the United States of America*. Tokyo, 1958. For the Japanese original, see *Mannen gannen daiichi kenbei shisetsu nikki*, Tokyo, 1977.

Nagao Masanori. *Fukuzawaya Yukichi no kenkyū*. Tokyo, 1988.

Nakajima Mineo. *Bakushin Fukuzawa Yukichi.* Tokyo, 1991.
Nihon gaikōshi jiten. Tokyo, 1992.
Nishikawa Shunsaku. *Fukuzawa Yukichi no yokogao.* Tokyo, 1998.
————. *Fukuzawa Yukichi to sannin no koshintachi.* Tokyo, 1985.
Nishikawa Shunsaku and Matsuzaki San'ichi, eds. *Fukuzawa Yukichi no hyakunen.* Tokyo, 1999.
Nishikawa Shunsaku and Nishizawa Naoko, eds. *Fudangi no Fukuzawa Yukichi.* Tokyo, 1998.
Numata Jirō and Matsuzawa Hiroaki, eds. *Seiyō kenbunshū. Nihon shisō taikei* series. Tokyo, 1974.
Olney, Jessie. *A Practical System of Modern Geography.* Hartford, CN, 1830.
Phillips, Richard. *An Easy Grammar of Geography.* Boston, 1807.
Rainichi seiyō jinmei jiten. Tokyo, 1983.
Ripley, George, and Charles A. Dana, eds. *The New American Cyclopaedia: A Popular Dictionary of General Knowledge.* 16 vols. New York, 1865.
Robertson, William. *The Works of William Robertson.* London, 1827.
Rosovsky, Henry. *Capital Formation in Japan.* Glencoe, IL, 1961.
Sashi Tsutae. "Shippitsu memo mitsukaru." *Mita Hyōron,* August–September 1991.
Smith, Adam. *Lectures on Jurisprudence.* Oxford, 1978.
————. *Lectures on Justice, Police Revenue, and Arms.* Oxford, 1896.
Smith, Roswell C. *Geography: Geography on the Productive System.* Philadelphia, 1835.
Stafford, H. G. *General Geography and Rudiments of Useful Knowledge.* Hudson, NY, 1809.
Sugiyama, Chūhei, and Hiroshi Mizuta. *Enlightenment and Beyond.* Tokyo, 1988.
Tamaki Norio. *Kigyōka Fukuzawa Yukichi no shōgai.* Tokyo, 2002.
Tanaka Akira. *Kindai Nihon no ayunda michi.* Tokyo, 2005.
————. *Mikan no Meiji ishin.* Tokyo, 1979.
Tomita Masafumi. *Kōshō Fukuzawa Yukichi.* 2 vols. Tokyo, 1992.
Tōyama Shigeki. *Fukuzawa Yukichi, shisō to seiji to no kanren.* Tokyo, 1977.
Turgot, Anne-Robert-Jacques. *Turgot on Progress, Sociology, and Economics: A Philosophical Review of the Successive Advances of the Human Mind, on Universal History [and] Reflections on the Formation and Distribution of Wealth.* Trans. and ed. R. L. Meek. Cambridge, Eng., 1973.
Tytler, Alexander Fraser. *Elements of General History, Ancient and Modern.* Concord, NH, 1909.
Uete Michiari, *Nihon kindai shisō no keisei.* Tokyo, 1974.
van Gulik, R. H. "Kakkaron, a Japanese Echo of the Opium War," *Monumenta Serica* 4 (1939–1940).
Watanabe Hiroshi. *Kinsei Nihon shakai to Sōgaku.* Tokyo, 1985.
Wayland, Francis. *Elements of Moral Science,* ed. J. L. Blau. Cambridge, 1963.
————. *Elements of Political Economy.* Boston, ca. 1841.
Woodbridge, William C. *Rudiments of Geography.* Hartford, CT, 1821.
————. *A System of Universal Geography, Ancient and Modern.* Hartford, CT, 1824.
Worcester, Joseph E. *Elements of Geography, Ancient and Modern.* Boston, 1819.
Yamaguchi Kazuo. *Fukuzawa Yukichi no Amerika taiken.* Tokyo, 1986.
Yasukawa Junnosuke. *Fukuzawa Yukichi to Maruyama Masao.* Tokyo, 2003.

Illustration Sources and Credits

189

Index

191

the West *(continued)*
  and Meiji reforms, 121; military of, 9, 82,
  143; as model, 103–107, 134; otherness
  of, 161–162; science from, 4–5, 6; stages
  in, 1, 34, 35–36, 37, 103–107, 108, 134,
  146, 150–151, 157, 182n77; as threat,
  131–138. See also *Conditions in the West*
Western learning, 5, 6–7, 80–81, 132, 133,
  163–164
Westernization: and Fukuzawa, 100, 101,
  110; governmental component of, 146,
  148–150; intellectual component of, 146,
  147–148; and Japan *vs.* China, 113;

popular response to, 146, 147–148;
  resistance to, 107–110
Whigs, 27, 76
William of Orange, 13
women, 23, 70, 73, 147, 162; and stages, 37,
  45, 48, 52, 58
Woodbridge, William Channing, 36–38
Worcester, Joseph Emerson, 35–36, 172n8
Wright, Nathaniel, 172n4

yin-yang, 155, 156, 158
Yoshida Shōin, 149

Zhu Xi, 6, 62, 63, 175n9

www.ingramcontent.com/pod-product-compliance
Lightning Source LLC
Chambersburg PA
CBHW031614310326
41914CB00126B/1783/J